HYPNOTISING THE CAT

(and other squibs)

Mike Harding

HYPNOTISING THE CAT
(and other squibs)

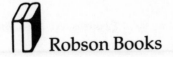

Robson Books

First published in Great Britain in 1995 by
Robson Books Ltd.
Bolsover House
5-6 Clipstone Street
London W1P 8LE

ISBN 0 86051 994 5

*Printed in Great Britain by St Edmundsbury Press, Bury St
Edmunds, Suffolk*

Thanks to Mr. Mike Unger (or, as my spell checker reads him Mr. 'Mighty Underwear') of the Manchester Evening News for encouraging me to do all this in the first place and thanks to our cat who gave me the idea for the title

Contents

Hypnotising the Cat

● ● ● ● ● ● ● ● ● ● ● ● ● ● ● ● ● ● ●

Hypnotising the Cat

Introduction

A long time ago the editor of the Manchester Evening News *Mr. Mighty Underwear found me in a tired and emotional state after the* Guardian *and* Manchester Evening News *Drama Awards and, plying me with folding beer tokens with Her Majesty's head printed on them, he inveigled me into writing a weekly column for the* Manchester Evening News.

As somebody who found homework a distasteful affair and an infringement of liberty that should have been cited under the Geneva Convention I then found myself having to write a thousand words every week. It was like being in detention for something I hadn't done. So every week come rain or rain, without fail I churned out my thousand words on my little Apple Macintosh lap-top. I tapped them out on planes high above the American Mid West, in motel rooms in North Carolina and in smoky rooms in the West and North of Ireland. I have annoyed passengers on the Inter City by tapping away at the little plastic keys and almost drowning out the noise of them gibbering down their mobile phones telling somebody to sell gold and buy lead and that they'd be home soon and she could put the Coq au Vin in the Neff.

The column is generally accepted with a modicum of favour though any reference to the Queen or the Pope usually calls forth torrents of abuse from anonymous letter writers. I often picture them sat at their tables dipping the Bic in vitriol, tongues firmly jammed in the corners of their mouths, heads bent over the Basildon Bond as they try to find words foul enough to hurl at me. 'Shite' was for long a favourite, only having been replaced recently by 'bollocks'. One aberrant from the norm of epistolatory rotten eggthrowers called me 'shite on legs', which is a North East expression. I can only assume that some Catholic Loyalist Geordie got blown off course on his annual migration south from the leek fields of Jarrow to the beaches of Ibiza and fetched up in Eccles or Mumps or some such place.

Some of the material in this book is loosely based on those articles, and although it has a Northern flavour, I see that as no bad thing. For too long the South has seen itself as the omphalos of all things cultural and the present-day Bloomsbury set of Amis, Rushdie, Barnes and Kureshi are held up as examples to us all. Were I a letter writer I would reply 'Bollocks, they are shites on legs'.

But I am not a letter writer I am merely a hack who feels it well past time that the North's own Bloomsbury Group was recognised. What of Arnold Crunchbucket, author of Camels to the Pole or Elphinstone Drinkpootle, whose seminal work, The World of Grommets Vols. 1 to 23, has earned him the admiration of small-bore central heating engineers the world over?

However I digress.

On with the motley, vaseline your eyes and if you have tears to shed then prepare to shed them now. Never will your flabber have been so gasted.

● ●

The Ghost of Christmas Exercised

So that's it, another one gone. The ashtrays of life brimmeth over and lo there are but the lees left to drink as we move another year closer to shuffling off this mortal coil.

I'm sure I'm not alone. You know the feeling. 'What was all that about?' I say as I stare around me at a mini Everest of wrapping paper and holly and carry another box full of jingling empties to the recycling bin. Another one gone, another haze of crazy days of cheese nibbles, soggy crisps, sausages that look like dogs' willies, cans of warm Australian kangaroo urine and glasses of Italian antifreeze gone down the great plug-hole of Time. And the questions that are asked when it is all over and the reckoning is to pay.

Did I really spend Christmas Day with a mad paper hat on, staring across the ruins of a turkey at Ken the crypto-fascist brother-in-law, listening to him go on about how '... at least Maggie sorted the unions out'? And did I really keep quiet when my mother nudged me with her free elbow and gave me one of her warning looks as she passed with the gravy jug?

What am I going to do with eight bottles of Old Spice and six ties of such amazing psychadelicness that they could induce epilepsy in a mole?

Who was that woman who pinched my bum in The Duke's '92 Pub on Christmas Eve?

There are other questions, too, more to do with what the Anglo Saxons used to call 'agenbite of inwit', an enquiry into the state of my soul I suppose you could call it. It must be Christmas that brings it on.

Why do I carry on drinking when I know full well from years of experience that in the morning I'm going to wake up with a head like a box of hot frogs and a tongue that is so covered in fur and garlic it feels as though I've been licking the back axle of a Greek village bus? And why can't I be gracious enough to wear the bloody awful socks from Maureen and Eamonn and the mustard-yellow cardigan my mother has knitted me yet again? And why am I so snobbish that the present from Uncle John, a brass gadget shaped like a guitar made for hanging keys on, will never be screwed to the wall in the hall?

And so much of Christmas now seems hazy and half-real. I have vague memories of being thrown out of Mulligan's Irish Pub on Christmas Eve. I was not alone. The entire pub was sent out into the frost that lay about crisp and even to gather winter fuel at seven o'clock or something like. 'Why are you closing at this strange hour?' a foolhardy imbiber enquired of mine host. Back came a reply which must go down as the Yuletide quote of all time. 'It's Christmas. F..k off home!' An unusual benison but one that I must say was not taken unkindly by the gathered motley.

About the rest of the evening I have little or no memory at all. The long-haired person who cohabits with me tells me that when I eventually did arrive home I sat in the chair and gibbered; she has had, so she says, more exciting Christmas Eves and better conversation out of a bowl of Rice Krispies. The whole week flew by in similar circumstances.

Did I really arm-wrestle a nun under the war memorial in St Peter's Square on Boxing Day? Did I really kiss a Scotsman dressed as Mr. Blobby on New Year's Eve? Only He whose birthday we were celebrating will know and he ain't telling.

Who the blinky heck is Mr. Blobby anyway? I know what he looks like. Bernard Manning with chicken pox. But what is he? I sometimes feel as though I've flown in on a scout ship from some other planet. I know that in the last

year I've spent four months abroad and the rest of the year
has been taken up pretty much with writing and touring,
doing gigs and readings and moving house, so that conse-
quently I haven't watched much television - but that
shouldn't make me feel like a creature from the planet
Teflon.

● ●

Enter an Egyptian Doctor Covered in Cat Poo

Truth is not just stranger than fiction - it's a damn
sight funnier too. I started writing a play earlier this
year based around a family reunion at Christmas
and I got stuck. Not with the creation of the characters but
with the plot. The characters were no real problem because
I did what I always do and plundered the family vaults
and my web of friends and acquaintances for eccentric
and/or lustful uncles, neurotic cousins, bawdy grandads
and forgetful aunts. It's a lot easier writing about people
you know than it is trying to make up characters out of thin
air, though you generally don't use the whole person in
case you get sued or written out of various wills. You do
what Frankenstein did when he created his monster in
Ingolstadt and use bits and pieces of people to make a new
one. Hair colour from Uncle Ben, ability to repeat the same
boring story about how he fought against Rommel in
North Africa four times in the course of an evening from
Cousin Paddy, and meanness and a tendency to hide
bottles of booze (which are free anyway) under beds and
in airing cupboards from cousin Pete, and there you have
it, a whole new person who I'll call Cousin James. Add a

cardigan and a panatela cigar, a silly paper hat and four cans of Boddington's draught bitter and you have the beginnings of a person. Characters are no real problem. The plot's the thing.

You see, generally we're no longer interested in the kinds of things Shakespeare (the maestro of the plot) wrote about - Julius Caesar, Hamlet, Macbeth. We just wouldn't write those kind of plays today. Nobody invites kings to stay at their castles and murders them nowadays, they just sell their taped telephone conversations and photographs of their ex-wives in lycra at the gym to the *Daily Mirror*.

Nowadays, instead of King Lear being dispossessed by his daughters and ending up raving mad but heroic on a blasted heath in a thunderstorm he'd be packed off to some twilight home to sit by the radiator dribbling on his zimmer frame. The stuff of epic has gone and all our heroes are small beer. Which brings me to the point of my story - the plot. There I was on Christmas morning sitting in my daughter's house waiting for the turkey, gravy, daft hats and sprouts when the plot for my play fell out of the sky. My other daughter is a doctor working in a hospital in the Midlands. She is a pleasant girl and a good doctor who suffers from a malady common amongst doctors nowadays, an overwhelming urge to perform euthanasia on Virginia Bottomley. But let that rest for the moment. She is also single and asked us could she bring along a man friend from the hospital who would be alone for Christmas. Of course everybody said yes and so they arrived just before dinner on Christmas Day. There we were all sat in a sea of wrapping paper and sellotape when we heard the noise of their car arriving. Now my daughter the doctor has two cats, big overweight spoilt moggies called Huxley and Rueben, my other daughter has a dog called Mojo who has a pathological hatred of anything that isn't exactly like him - ie. a mongrel terrier of uncertain parentage. If there

Hypnotising the Cat

was a British Movement for dogs - he'd be in it. Cats are his main enemies and he delights in doing battle with them. My daughter with the cats felt guilty about leaving them alone on Christmas Day and brought them with her along with her friend, an Egyptian orthopaedic surgeon who I will call Sabri.

They were travelling from Dudley, an hour or so away in Sabri's elegant car. Ten minutes into the journey the cats voided their bowels on the back seat of the car. There are some things worse than cat poo but I haven't come across them yet. In the course of the next hour they voided their bowels a further three times. Sabri is a gentleman and carried on driving, eyes streaming, throat gagging, forbearing to mention the fact that the St Christopher medal on the dashboard was trying to get off. Just as the car arrived at the house the cats went for gold. Their little botties pressed up against the bars of their travelling basket, they sprayed the interior of the car and Sabri with what was left of their insides. His elegant blazer and the back of his head were re-sprayed an unfashionable shade of brown and as he entered the house and shook my hand his eyes were watering and his hands were shaking. We cleaned him up and gave him a glass of champagne as the cats were being hosed down and blow-dried in the bathroom. Half an hour later, as the turkey is about to be brought from the oven, two fluffy cats come into the living room and are attacked by a berserk Mojo, who underestimates the toughness of these two particular moggies. One of them scars his nose for life while the other takes a chunk out of his ear. Then both cats climb the curtains and sit on the pole spitting and glaring down at us all as Cousin Paddy, trying to make our guest feel at home says, 'I was in Egypt during the war Sabu - Eighth Army - we gave that Rommel a right pasting - mind you he were a good general I'll give him that', and on he drones as the dog is howling, the cats are spitting and Sabri is sitting there on his fifth glass of champagne staring glassy-eyed into the distance and the smoke from a burning turkey curls round the door. And every word is true. So my new play - *Tidings of Comfort and Joy* - now begins Act One, Scene One, Enter an Egyptian Doctor covered in cat poo.

• •

A Trip to Pagan Geordieland

So, all in all, that was Christmas then, the celebration of the birthday of a poor joiner who hadn't a half penny to scratch his Godly *derrière* with was celebrated as usual by the Greatest Spend on Earth. Weird really. But Gentle Reader, think not that I in my glass house am flinging feather dusters here. *Mea maxima* very much indeed *culpa* Pal. The Barclaycard melted with over-use, my arms grew at least another inch longer carrying all that 'stuff' and I've covered up all the mirrors in the house until I've been back down the gym and lost all this extra 'relaxed muscle'. Still, apart from the shell-shocked Egyptian gentleman covered in cat poo it was all fairly calm and pleasant and, like a lot of other families, we faced each other over the ruined carcass of a turkey wearing our daft hats and reading Christmas cracker jokes at each other until the Queen's speech. During the speech, we all fell asleep as is the family custom. We've seen the act before, she talks very nicely and all that but there are no jokes, she doesn't juggle or dance or anything and there's no supporting act. To tell the truth I'd rather watch Fry and Laurie - and that's saying something since they are to comedy what Crippen was to marriage guidance.

After the Queen it was time to get up and start eating and drinking again with the next lot of visitors on Christmas Day night. And so it went on day after day until the sight of a mince pie now threw me into hot sweats and the sound of cork popping had my liver knocking on my ribs in protest.

New Year's Eve we spent at Allendale in Northumberland. They have a fire festival there which is believed to date back to the pagan Baal fires of the North. Fifty men disguised in fancy dress carry blazing barrels of tar around the village on their heads in a long snaking procession. It's all terrifically atmospheric. The stars shine on the velvet dingle of the night, the tar barrels send their flames shooting into the black sky, lighting the whole village square, the brass band plays 'Blaydon Races' and 'Keep Your Feet Still Geordie Hinnie' and then on the stroke of midnight they toss the barrels on to a huge bonfire, all the windows of the houses in the square melt, dozens of cars lose their paint jobs, then everybody kisses everybody else and wishes them a happy New Year and runs round the bonfire for a bit. After that there is music, dancing and general mayhem until the early hours when everybody lurches to bed. The next day there is a lot of first-footing and singing until the New Year is well and truly christened and the Old Year nailed in its grave. It is all really wild but (being in Geordieland) is all very good humoured and pleasant. No trouble, no fights, no bottle throwing, just a lot of singing and dancing and drinking followed by a lot of thick heads and furry tongues.

I have travelled in Geordieland quite a lot and know a good few people up there that I am happy to call friends, though it took me a while to get to understand the accent: 'Howay man how's it gannin? Why ye knaw ah wuz supping the broon dog wi the lads doon the Cricketer's the neet stottin' doon the wa' hinny etc. etc.' When they made a survey on dialects a few years back they asked people to rate them out of ten for trustworthiness and the Geordie accent came top. It is a lovely accent with traces of Scandinavian still stuck in there and it's a great language for telling stories in too, and though I'm sure I can't do it justice I'll tell you one.

A couple of years ago a Geordie went to London to meet the Queen.

'How's it gannin' Geordie?' asked HM.

'Why canny Liz. The leeks have been great the year man! Wor Tommy won forst at the show ya knaw! How's the corgies?'

'Canny, Geordie lad. Would ye like a sup o' tea an' a bit cake?'

'Why ay man.'

'A meringue?'

'No yer nat wrang. I like cake!'

It may lose a lot in translation, it's hard to say.

Talking about New Year - do you ever wonder how they work out Leap Years and all that kind of stuff? I mean why do we have to have an extra day every four years? It seems a clumsy way of doing things really. And why are there sixty seconds in the minute and sixty minutes to the hour? Apparently that's something to do with the ancient Sumerians to whom sixty was a magical number. Twenty-four hours is something to do with the Romans, the months having anything from twenty-eight to thirty-one days in them is something to do with Nero's dog chewing up the calendar, and seven days to the week is something to do with the Lord's Day Observance Society. I think it would be easier if we had five-day weeks and only worked two of them. That would give us twice as many weekends and would soak up the army of the unemployed since we'd have to share out the jobs. Fourteen months of twenty-five days each would give us three hundred and fifty days a year so that without leap years we'd shift on a day or so each year in terms of the seasons. That would mean that after a while, a hundred and seventy-five years or so, there would be snow on midsummer's day and Christmas would happen in a heat wave. Then the whole thing would carry on for another hundred and seventy-five years until it was normal and it would all begin again. I think this is a very good idea and should be taken up immediately by the Adam Smith Institute along with all the other nonsense they come out with like twenty-four-lane double-decker motorways and VAT on old people's coal. Come to think of it, it's far too sensible an idea for the likes of them.

• •

Torture by Tie-Back

Mary Tudor said that when she died and they cut her open they would find the word 'Calais' carved on her heart - I think she'd had a bad meat pie there once and she'd thrown up on the ferry home and showed herself up in front of the bucket and spade brigade. I mean it can't be very nice if you're the Queen of England and all your loyal subjects are stood around eating their jellied eels and ice-cream, doing 'Knees Up Mother Brown' and 'Knocked 'Em in the Old Kent Road Cor Blimee!' and you've got your little crowned head over the rail feeding day-old carrots to the seagulls and soon-to-be canned sardines. It's bad enough being shot at by a starting pistol in Australia, and a deodorant in New Zealand - heaving your cornflakes up in front of four hundred pearly kings and queens on a day trip from the Isle of Dogs must be a terribly disnobling experience.

But if she had 'Calais' carved on her heart then I'll have 'Tie-backs' carved on mine. I hate Tie-backs! I hate them with an irrationality and obsession that is probably bordering on some sort of psychosis. All this is very subjective, I know, and some psychiatrist would probably have a field day if they got me in the chair, but to me tie-backs, like big knickers, hair lacquer and Reliant Robins, represent more than they are. They are symbols, they connote more than they denote, as Eric Einstein, brother of the more famous Sydney, once said as he swept up the hair, sat the little boys on planks and took bets in Macky Davis's barber's shop on Cheetham Hill Road. Reliant Robins always look to me like Formula One cheese wedges, and without any obvious connection they make me think of old sheds and allotments, Sloan's Liniment and dead flamingoes. Big knickers make me think of Southern Cemetery, keg beer and Bernard Manning. I offer no explanation for these phenomena, I merely observe them.

Tie-backs make me think of Barbara Cartland, Margaret Thatcher, heated hostess trolleys, warm Liebfraumilch, knitted poodle toilet-roll holders, bridge parties, gymkhanas and capital punishment. They embody everything I hate about the Little England mentality, the notion that the British are best at everything and that the English Middle Class are the best of the lot.

And, worst of all, last week the long-haired part of the relationship I am in decided that she wanted tie-backs for the new curtains. I ranted, cursed, reasoned, sulked, pretended I'd gone deaf - all to not the slightest effect. Like the Chinese Water Torture, where a little drop of water is dripped on to the forehead of a bound victim over a long period of time, until he eventually goes completely Harpic, the gradual pressure of this one-person tie-back lobby ground me down.

So last Saturday I got out the drill and checked the bit sizes against the stupid screws that have to be screwed in the wall to hold the hooks that the rotten stupid tie-backs hang from. Ha! I thought - saved! I don't have a bit the right size to drill the hole for the hooks to go into the wall so we can't hang the tie-backs up. And my car's in for a service so there's no way I can go to B&Q for a new bit.

Well, you probably remember that children's story about the pig that wouldn't jump over the stile for the old woman - it ended up something like 'Water water douse Fire, Fire won't burn Stick, Stick won't beat Dog, Dog won't bite Pig, Pig won't jump over stile and we won't get home this evening.' In our house last Saturday it began... 'Mike Mike phone Pete, Pete can bring Car, Car can drive to B&Q, B&Q can sell Bit and Rawlplugs, Bit can drill Hole, Hole can eat Rawlplug, Rawlplug can eat Screw, Screw can hold Hook, Hook can hold Tie- back and Mike might get a pint this evening.' But it ended up, 'Pete Pete bring back Car, Drill has bit Mike, Mike has Hole in hand, Car take Mike to Crumpsall Hospital, Doctor Doctor sew Hand, Nurse stick Tetanus Needle in Bum, Car Car go to Pub. Too late Pub shut.'

The worst thing was that when I got home the high priestess of soft furnishings had finished the job herself without any obvious signs of stigmata. I walked in looking hurt, sniffed and said 'The tie-backs look nice' and went to bed to read a book on first aid. I want to know what to do next time. It's no use standing there with a tea-towel wrapped around the injured part shouting, 'Emergency Emergency - This is not a drill! This is not a drill!' like they do in American films. She just looked at me as though I was stupid and said, 'It is a drill - It's a Black and Decker'. I hate it when she's right all the time.

• •

Lady Macbeth and the Shrink-Wrap Dagger

My hand is a bit better now so last weekend I had to put three shelves up in the minuscule cubby hole where we keep the vacuum cleaner and the mop bucket in the Harding flat in the Castle. Don't ask why - it was obviously 'shelf time' just as a few days ago it was 'tie-back time' and in a week or so it will be 'bathroom cabinet and spice rack time'. Now, I am to DIY what Nero was to fire-insurance, the very thought of drilling and banging makes me think of desert islands or a life on the open road with busted shoes, rags wrapped round my bunions and a red handkerchief tied on a stick over my shoulder. But I gave in. I don't know why but the type of feminism espoused by the long-haired part of this relationship doesn't stretch to Black and Deckers and electric screw-drivers so it was up to this foolhardy descendant of the mammoth hunter, wolf-killer and warrior to splash on the Givenchy woad and plug in the two -speed hammer watsit with the tungsten thingy doo dah. I measured the wall, drew lines with the aid of a spirit level, marked up the places for the screws, drilled the holes and stood back in the timeless pose that must have been invented by the earliest hunter when he threw the first slab of Dumbo sirloin down on the cave floor.

Then I picked up the shelf brackets. They were shrink-wrapped on thick pieces of card. It had taken me about a quarter of an hour to drill the eighteen holes for the six shelf brackets and that includes fighting with the vacuum cleaner, the Christmas tree lights and the mop to disentangle the lead of the electric drill from the bird's nest it had got into with the lights and the vacuum tube. It took me more than half an hour, three fingernails, the skin off most of my knuckles and one elbow and a lot of blood and sweat and cursing to get six simple shelf brackets out of their cling-wrap shell. You'd have more chance getting the truth about Arms to Iraq out of the Mad Granny of Grantham. There must be more people in the casualty units of hospitals because of shrink-wrapping than any other single cause. Scissors skidded off, knives slid through the polythene and stuck in my thumb. I tried ripping the card and failed, I tried flinging the packages at the wall, jumping on them and shouting the filthiest words I knew at them and still I couldn't get the little buggers out. I was reminded of those words of Shakespeare, you know, the ones about Man, 'What a work thing is Man- the paragon of animals' and all that stuff. It's obvious that they didn't have shrink-wrap in Shakespeare's day or Duncan would still be alive in Act 7 with Macbeth stood outside the bedchamber, sweating and cursing and splitting his nails. You can just imagine it (well you can if you've got a mind like mine).

The murder scene from Macbeth by W .Shakespeare Gent (with help from M.H. Gent.)

Macbeth
Is this a dagger that I see before me
The handle stretched towards my outstretched hand?
Come let me clutch thee - 's blood! The thing is wrapped
In sodding shrink-wrap. Come! Off, off you - aargh!
Another nail is gone! I'll never play
The banjo again! This packaging will prove
The curse of all Mankind, some Satan's scheme
To drive us roundst the bend.
(*Throws dagger away*)
            Oh bugger it
I'll do him with the garden shears instead.

Lady Macbeth
My lord, dost not remember I did lend
Them Banquo for to clip the hedge... etc. etc.

Anyway the upshot was that I got the stuff off and put the
shelves up and they were all cockeyed, sloping to the left
at an angle of thirty degrees or so. I must be the only failed
DIY enthusiast with a square bubble in his spirit level. I've
got to do them all again but not until I've taken some
psycho-chemical designer drugs.

• •

The Vicar, the Watering Can and the Leprechaun's Gusset

I discovered the other day that most of my underpants
have been turned into dusters by the long-haired person who shares the house with me. I was a bit annoyed,
I was quite attached to some of them. The paisley jockey
shorts my Great Aunt Julia bought me for my 21st birthday
and the boxer shorts with the slogan 'Over the Hill but not
over the Hump' that the roadies gave me one Christmas
will be sorely missed. However, rather than start another
war I left her polishing the coal scuttle with my memories
and set off for the metropolis to buy some new shreddies.
And it struck me as I wandered round goggling in the
windows of the shops how boring men's underwear is. I
mean without being sexist about it, most women's' underwear is designed to be sexy - or at least to move things
about a bit. Men's underwear seems to be there just to stop
zips and seams causing rashes and watery eyes - in other

words it is purely functional. I think this is unfair - why can't men have sexy underwear too? I read somewhere that in Elizabethan times men wore codpieces to accentuate their bits. Apparently women would swoon in the street at the sight of these codpiece things. This seems a good idea to me. We didn't have any cod so I got a pair of Craster kippers out of the fridge and wandered round town with them tucked down the front of my jeans. Not one single interested glance did I get from any of the ladies on the street, though by the end of the afternoon I did have the undivided attention of three hundred and twenty-six cats and a black-headed gull.

In my search for something sexy or novel to wear under my everyday clothes I saw something in one shop I thought had gone out years ago. String underwear. Now string underwear is not sexy. It is anti-sex. It is to sex what Nero was to house insurance. I used to know somebody who wore string underwear. I saw him once stood there in nothing but his string underpants, not exactly something to stir the fires of lust in a feminine bosom - his bits looked like an undernourished perch in a keep net. In the end I went, as I always do, to Marks and Sparks and bought some serviceable but boring boxer shorts. I did think about buying some yellow dusters and sewing them together to make a couple of pairs but I don't think the demon cleaner would have seen the joke somehow.

I'm often asked if I find it hard to write my little bits and pieces of gibberish - 'You know,' they say, 'Finding something different to write about all the time.' To be honest sometimes I do. I sit there looking at a screen that is as blank as my mind, feeling totally uninspired, thinking, 'What can I write about. I mean nothing's happened. It's just been like last week. A bit of a drink on Wednesday. Went for a walk Thursday. Worked on my major novel on Friday for an hour.' All that sort of thing. After an eternity of sitting staring at the screen I get up and make myself a cup of tea and sit down and stare at it again. Then I make notes, random words that might inspire me. 'Watering cans - vicar - gusset - leprechaun,' that sort of thing. I stare at the words for an hour trying to make something from them - but nothing happens. Then I walk round the room breathing deeply to suppress a feeling of rising panic that is gripping me - the certainty that I will never write another word, that I am struck by that most fearsome disease: 'writer's block'. Then I think of Dostoevsky sat alone in his freezing cold garret in St Petersburg, the candle guttering, a dewdrop hanging from the end of his nose, the ink freezing on the quill as he scraped out his thousand words for the *St Petersburg Bugle* in between scribbling out the *Brothers Karamazov* and I think - if he can do it then so can I. And I force myself back to the little Apple and bang out the second thing that comes into my head. The first is always too dirty.

So here it is. In Dublin last week I heard the following story sworn to be true. Late one night two *gardai* (Irish police) noticed a car being driven in an erratic fashion along O' Connell Street. The car mounted the pavement scattering late night revellers, spun around, reversed into a shop doorway and set off again very wobbly going the wrong way up a one-way street. The *gardai* gave chase and pulled the car over. A pair of blood-shot eyes glared at them through the window. 'Do you mind stepping out of the car sir,' they said, opening the door. The man, an old farmer type with a flat hat and wellies, fell out on the pavement, pulled himself up by one of the *garda's* legs and asked them what they wanted. 'We've reason to believe you have been drinking.' they said. 'Drinking is it?' he replied. ' I've been at a wake and I've been drinking for two days. I wouldn't light a match near me if I was you.'

So the *gardai* produced the Bobby's Balloon and asked him to blow into it. It turned forty shades of green.

The *gardai* cautioned him and told him they were arresting him.

'What for?' he asked.

'Drunk driving,' they answered.

'I'm not driving,' the farmer replied, pointing to his wife who had been sat there quietly all the time at the wheel of the car which was a left hand drive Volvo. 'She's driving - she hasn't had a drop. Isn't it the bloody awful driver she is?'

And like I said, everybody in Dublin swore it was true - so it must be.

• •

I Dub Thee Sir Michael Pommie Comic

This may be the last time you read a book like this written by my good, bad and indifferent self. You see, the long-haired side of the partnership I am involved in has just entered two competitions that come through the letterbox and will win us a quarter of a million pounds in the comfort of our armchairs. One is something to do with *Which* magazine, the other is that *Reader's Digest* one with the car key in it that fits the car you might win just as a taster on your way up to the oodles of lolly. Having won a jar of apricots in brandy and a busy lizzie cutting at the local parish Brownies Winter Sale, she feels this is her lucky year and is now confident that half a million and an Audi is coming our way and I can throw away guitar, camera and Apple Mac and think about that cottage on the west coast of Kerry that I've dreamed about for so long. She's actually promised to split it down the middle and in her daydreams she's already spent some of it paying off the mortgage and the overdraft, driving down to the Nat

West in her brand new white Audi like one of the characters in the old *Film Fun* comic, beeping her horn and throwing a fistful of notes at Paul, the manager, when he comes out. He then falls over with a big balloon above his head with the word 'Swoon!!' written in it. She throws her cigar out of the window and drives off in a cloud of dust leaving him grovelling on the pavement.

As for my daydreams, I've got my painter's smock on and have just taken a break from the Turneresque apocalyptic seascape I am working on and am in Gussie Connor's bar in Doolin speaking fluent Irish to the neighbours (having taken lessons from the best professor in the land) while a peat fire burns in the old grate and a pint of wonderful real Guinness lies at my elbow. A fiddler strikes up and a torrent of blistering complicated reels (having taken lessons from the best professor in the land) flies from my banjo like bullets from a Chicago Piano on St Valentine's Day, if you don't mind the old metaphors getting a bit mixed up.

Ah well, as Prospero once said , 'We are such stuff as dreams are made on'. In other words - 'Don't give up the day job.'

I've often wondered what I'd do if I were ennobled. Apart from the fact that my grandmother would turn in her Fenian grave and my grandfather's ghost, assuming the shape of Keir Hardie, would haunt me through Kendals and Waterstones, finally forcing me to recant over the cotton boxer shorts in Marks and Spencers, I wouldn't know what to call myself. Lord Mike of Crumpsall sounds like Lord Snooty and His Pals, Lord Harding of the Irk Valley is a bit too strong. I think Sir Michael de Crumpsall is about right, though I would still like to be known to the lads and lassies as plain Sir Mike. And then there's 'droit de seigneur' of course, which as a noble I would then be allowed to exercise. In fact as soon as I find out what 'droit de seigneur' means, I'm certainly going to exercise it. I can hear Lady Harding now, shouting down from the turret, 'Take out that droit de seigneur now and exercise it before it craps on the carpet.'

There aren't many things that make me want to commit murder. I'm normally fairly placid (well, I do sort of foam at the mouth about the Americanisation of our culture and a few other things) but yesterday I had to go and bang my head against the wall and count to ten zillion. The long-haired side of the relationship had decided without consultation or forewarning to reorganise my CD collection. Now I actually like it jumbled. I like the fact that Peter Gabriel is next to Vivaldi, that Charlie Mingus nestles in between The Chieftains and Buddy Holly, while Dire Straits and Hank Williams sandwich a little known but ever so interesting Liverpool group called Half-Man, Half-Biscuit.

I knew where things were. In that chaotic jumble I could lay my hands in seconds on Stockton's Wing or Charlie Parker, knew that Brecht's *Threepenny Opera* was beside Gene Vincent's Greatest Hits and that Sweet Honey in the Rock was next to Nanci Griffiths and Christy Moore. Now it's all in alphabetical order and I can't find a pigging thing. Not content with turning all my old underpants into dusters and binning my Viz collection, she now has to savage my entire lifestyle and turn my treasured music collection into a sterile and ordered wasteland. Now the Shadows are next to Springsteen and Bo Diddley is next to the Bundhu Boys ... just a minute - Diddley begins with a 'd'! Ah, but of course Bo begins with a 'b' so I suppose that's all right then. As soon as she's gone off to her formation-swimming and welding classes I'm going to get all the CDs out, muddle them all up and put them back blindfolded. Given a couple of years I should be able to work out where they all are. And at least it won't be any worse than Diddley under 'b' for Bo.

I'm no wine buff, I couldn't tell you where a Chardonnay grape comes from or what makes a Sémillon not a Vouvray, but I do know what I like and what I like most at the moment are the Cook's Bay and Butterfly Ridge wines that come all the way from the land of *Neighbours, Home and Away* and other high cultural affairs. In the early eighties I was in Australia working and my memory of the Ozzy wines then was that they were, in the main, pretty bad. I actually went on a wine tasting in the Barossa valley near Adelaide and it was one of the most bizarre experiences of my life. The Barossa was largely peopled by German Lutheran refugees who emigrated to Australia, bringing their wine-growing skills with them and found the soil perfect for growing vines. We drove out of Adelaide and through the bush with scrub and desert all about us - GABA our guide called it - 'Great Australian Bugger All'. Coming round a hill we saw before us a massive Schloss, a German baronial castle that looked as though it had been flown over from the Bavaria of Mad Ludwig. Then we saw another one and another, and we noticed that standing in front of them were little fat men in *lederhosen* playing accordions and big-busted ladies in Tyrolean blouses waving and singing. The whole place was like a hot and dusty Dortmund, and the picture was made even more surreal when a group of aborigines wandered down the road singing a country and western song. We got out of the car feeling drunk already and went into one of the vine-yard's tasting rooms. I don't know whether they weren't keeping the wines long enough in those days or whether they hadn't got the mix of grapes right but they were raw and basic, the whites like battery acid, the reds like Cherryade. I was writing a series of articles for the *Guardian* at the time and in that week's article I described the wines as 'young with a hint of gum boot'.

Hypnotising the Cat

I was home ten days later when the article came out and I'd forgotten all about it when I was shown a cutting from one of Oz's big daily papers. Apparently the paper was not remotely amused by my wine appreciation. It was the headline though that gave me most amusement - 'Pommie Comic Rubbishes Oz Plonk'.

●●●●●●●●●●●●●●●●●●●●●

Saint Uncle Harry and the Sacred Hot Spring of Droylsden

You can choose your friends but not your family, somebody once said and how right that is. We're all stuck with what, for better or worse, the Kismet Futures and Fortunes Group PLC have dished out to us as relatives. If a friend gets on your bosom ends then you can either tell them so/move out of the neighbourhood/change your name or refuse to answer the phone whenever it rings. But family is different, blood runs thicker than Guinness so they say, and beyond doing a Stephen Fry, there's not much you can do about Cousin Alf and his collection of spam tin labels 1943-7 or Great Uncle Roger and his photographic memory of anything that happened before 1953 and his belief that all good music ended with Ruby Murray, Joe Loss and the Wobbly Cork All Star Women's Orchestra. Luckily I am blessed with a particularly good and unspectacular family who give me little grief, though I suspect being related to a man who makes a living talking about bums and willies and who once sat on a stuffed Alsatian dog on *Top of the Pops* has given them more than their just share of headaches at work and school.

Hypnotising the Cat

'Ey John. I saw your kid on the telly last night. How did you end up with a prat like that as a brother?'

Apart from my mother we don't have any real eccentrics in the family. I mean, what do you say to a woman who still wants to go hang gliding and learn Esperanto even though she's never been higher than Blackpool Tower and actually thinks that there is a country somewhere called Esperantenstein? I've tried to tell her the truth and have explained countless times that Esperanto is a total invention, that there is no country or race that has it as its native language and that it is spoken mainly by strange men in raincoats who lurk on the fringes of the train-spotting and 'Bacon wrote Shakespeare' fraternities, and ladies in tweed skirts who know a good recipe for nettle quiche and are related to people who have been abducted by aliens in flying saucers and hidden in the Great Pyramid of Cheops.

Thinking about it in the warm light of dawn, though, it does seem that my mother is not the only eccentric in the family. Uncle Harry rises above the normal in many respects. Harry the Carpet, as he is known in certain parts of this city, was at one time the Godfather of Cheetham Hill. Before he went into the carpet business and became respectable, he ran the notorious Ghatkis Gang responsible for the fake bagel-smuggling ring that flourished there in the seventies. Fake bagels flooded the market and it was only when some of his runners were kneecapped by Reuben Hood, Mackie Davies and the Tobias Gang that he went legit and turned from covering North Manchester in fake bagels to covering floors with foam back, tufted and imitation Axminster. 'Even the Queen is using this in Buckingham Palace now, love. Won't have the old stuff now. The corgis have ruined it.' I worked for Uncle Harry for a while and books could be written about it, though until I get a good libel lawyer they will not be. One Christmas Eve he sent us out to the wilds of Droylsden to fit a hall stairs and landing. Pointing out to him that it was half past four and that Bob Cratchit and Tiny Tim were going to stand us a pint of Stingo in the Griffin Alehouse across the way and that I still had the turkey to buy was to no avail and off I went. It took a long time to fit the carpet because the stairs were awkward and there was a great deal of cutting and tucking to be done. At six thirty I was still there sweating and cutting and tacking. Enter Uncle Harry to see how things were going.

'Stand back,' he says, 'and let an expert at the job.'

Raising an expert hammer on high he expertly drove a two-inch nail through a one inch floorboard. Now Plank's Law states that 'a two-inch nail going through one-inch floorboard has an extra inch that must go somewhere', while Einstein's Third Law of Thermodynamics states 'Central heating pipes should be laid under floorboards wherever possible since laying them on top of floorboards leads to unsightly lumps in the carpet that can trip up small children and the infirm.' Uncle Harry had been on the Classics side at school and was more conversant with Aeschylus and Virgil than Einstein and Plank. So his expert nail went expertly through a copper hot-water pipe. From the middle of a red rose in the landing carpet there suddenly sprang a magical hot spring.

'A Blessed Miracle,' I shouted, 'Hail St Harry, discoverer of the famous Christmas Eve Hot Holy Well of Droylsden.' He was not amused, particularly since discovering a Holy Plumber who would come out at that time on a Christmas Eve and block up the Holy Well proved damn near impossible. And the lady of the house, surrounded by over-excited children and up to her armpits in turkey's bum was not happy either when drops of hot water trickled through the kitchen ceiling on to her head.

I was reading *The Young Conservative's Book of Knowledge* the other day. It's quite a slim book, in fact you can get through all of its four pages in a matter of minutes. Under the heading, 'Useful cliches every prospective Tory candidate should know, I read, 'Cleanliness is next to Godliness.' A load of rubbish. I looked in the dictionary and 'Cleanliness' is next to 'Cleavage'. 'Godliness' is next to 'goldfish' and 'go-cart'.

●●●●●●●●●●●●●●●●●●●●●●

Very Grim Fairy Tales

I was reading a fairy story to a small person of my acquaintance the other night when it suddenly struck me that what I was reading was not just horrific; it seems that to most children of today living in the world of the television and the Information Superhighway, they are also quite frankly weird and bizarre.

I began by announcing that the story was called *Hansel and Gretel*.

'Is there a princess in it?'

'No, but it's a really good story.'

'I like princesses.'

'Well, Gretel is a little girl who sort of becomes a princess.'

'I'm going to be a princess when I grow up.'

I began reading and soon the small person had stopped wittering on about princesses and was listening, thumb in mouth, eyes looking dreamily into space. I had just got to the part where the mother and father are trying to lose the children for the second time and the children have laid a trail of breadcrumbs behind them so that they can find their way home and the stupid birds have come and eaten it all up when the small voice asked:

Hypnotising the Cat

'Why did the mummy and daddy want to leave them in the woods?'

'Well er ... they were poor and they had no food for them ... and erm ... well I suppose they hoped that somebody would find them and look after them.'

'No they didn't! They wanted them to be killdid and eatid up by wulfs.'

'No I don't think so ... I mean it may have been at the back of their minds but I'm sure that wasn't why they really did it.'

'I think their mummy and daddy should have been killdid and eatid up by wulfs.'

'Possibly - now do you want to hear some more of the story or not?'

'Yes.'

'Right then.'

'If they were my mummy and daddy I would have rundid away to gwanmas.'

I carried on for a while with various muttered interjections about 'gwanmas' and 'mummies and daddies being killdid dead!' until I got to the Gingerbread House. 'And there in a clearing was a great cottage made all of gingerbread and sweets. Its roof was made of icing sugar and the windows were made of crystal sugar and the path was made of caramel whirls'.

'What about the gawidge?'

'They didn't have a garage.'

'Why didn't they have a gawidge?'

'Because the lady who lives there is a witch and she doesn't have a car like mummy and daddy, she rides around on a broomstick.'

'Where does she keep her bwoomstick?'

'In a broomstick garage made of marzipan with a liquorice up-and-over door and barley-sugar windows.' I knew when I was beaten.

'So Hansel went past the garage and crept towards

the cottage ever so slowly and tore a piece off the roof and began to eat it hungrily.'

'He was norty Hansel. He will get smacked now.'

'For eating the roof?'

'No, because he is going to get bad teeth and the dentist will make holes in his head with a grill brrrrrmrmrmrmr!!! Oww ! Oww! he will shout and it will serve him right. Has he got a teethbross?'

'Probably.'

'Where?'

'It'll be in his pocket.'

'Let me see.'

She pulled the book towards her and peered at the picture.

'I can't see it.'

'It's folded up. It's one of those travelling tooth-brushes and you can fold it up and put it in your pocket. Shall I read some more?'

'Where's the toothpaste?'

'Gretel's got it down her stocking. Now sit up and we'll get to the exciting part soon because the witch comes.'

'I don't like witches.'

I carried on to the accompaniment of low mutterings about witches and what a certain small person would do if they saw a witch and from what she was saying it seemed lucky for the witches that they hadn't yet come into contact with this particular inquisitor.

'And just as Hansel was reaching up to tear off one of the jelly babies round the window frame for Gretel there was a sudden shriek and an old lady came round the corner...'

'Is she the witch?'

'Yes.'

'Where's her picture?'

I showed her a picture that looked for all the world like Baroness Thatcher without benefit of hairbrush, make-up or orthodontist and the child shuddered.

'That's a horrible witch.'

'Yes, it is.'

'Well, Hanstel and Grekkul should go to the phone and ring the number.'

'What number?'

'The number for children to ring when their mummies and daddies or other people are norty to them. It's an oh hate undred number.'

'Oh.'

'It's in the book. I sordid it on telly.'

'And that will get rid of the witch, will it?'

'Yes the pleecemans will rest her and take her to jail.'

'But there isn't a phone! See there's no wires.'

There was a moment's pause, then the small person knelt up on the sofa and dragged the book from my hands. She scanned the picture looking for Telecom cables fastened somewhere to one of the liquorice allsorts that were used as corbels on the gable end.

'That's a silly story.' And that was that, the small person wanted no more. Gingerbread House - yes, Wicked Witch - no problem, no phone - forget it.

'Do you want another one?'

'What's it about?'

'It's called the Princess and the Phone.'

'All right then.'

And I made up some nonsense about a princess whose phone breaks down and a frog comes to mend it and he tells her that he's really a prince and that a wicked witch has turned him into a frog telephone engineer ... but before I got to the interesting part where she kisses him and he turns back into a prince telephone engineer the small person was asleep and I was ready for a big drink. Why is everything so hard nowadays?

● ●

Love Lust and Loose Livers

S pring is sprung, the lambs are gambolling and young men's fancies are turning to thoughts of may poles, comely milkmaids and a spot of Hey Nonny No. At least they did in the glorious past. Once the cold blast of winter had stopped shrinking important bits to the size of acorns and it was safe enough to get them out again, off would come the flannel vest with the brown paper and the goose grease the young maidens had been sewn into all winter, and it was into the meadows to crush a few butter-cups with their bums and celebrate the solstice with a bit of Fall de Al de Riddle and Right Roll the Diddle Aye Do. At least that's what almost every English folk song tells us. Don't take my word for it, go look at the *English Book of Penguin Folk Songs* and there you will see it in cold print.

Two thirds of the songs start off with:

'As I rode out one sweet May morning' ...
or ... *'Twas early one May morning as I walked o'er the grass.'*

They then go on to spend the rest of verse one describing how they meet somebody of the opposite sex, verse two is spent exchanging names and talking about hobbies and the weather and by verse three they are doing rudies. (Foreplay was not invented until 10:32 pm November 22nd 1947). There are hundreds of songs like this through-out the British Isles composed from the sixteenth century until just after the Second World War. But I have to say, I wonder what a present-day folk song would look like:

*'Twas very late one May evening I went down to the disco
I dropped some acid, took some "E" and sniffed a load of Bisto'*
(You may laugh but how do you know that the youth of today are not into gravy-browning abuse? Who would

have thought years ago that anybody would have got off on sniffing glue? Glue in them there days was made not of solvents but of boiled-down fish bone. What a wonderful time you would have had sniffing that lot. You'd have been better off sticking your head down a Portuguese fisherman's welly.)

But to get back to the point - where are the folk songs of today? Does anybody sing songs like the following (to the tune of the 'Lincolnshire Poacher')

'I am a rambling accountant from jolly Lincolnshire
With my Papermate pen I've rambled round for many's the long year,
I gets me clothes from Next 'cos they're smart and not very dear
And 'tis my delight on a Friday night to drink some Budweiser beer.'

I think not.

What kind of heritage are the future kids of these islands going to have anyway? I saw on the *South Bank Show* that we are about to be taken over by a craze for American Country Music and Line dancing. Now I like that kind of stuff where it is - in America. I've been to the Grand Old Oprey and Elvis's Graceland and I've been to Conway Twitty's Record Store and very nice they all are too, but that (in my humble opinion) is where they should stay, securely across the pond. But I suppose they won't, I suppose we'll end up with them here like McDonalds and Coca-Cola and Power Rangers. It does so make me laugh when I hear people going on about being British. We stopped being British when there were no longer twelve pennies to the shilling and petrol didn't come in gallons. We are now the fifty-third state of the United States and we'd better get on with it. In my case I'm going to buy a Stetson, some cowboy boots and a frilly shirt, learn to line dance and start writing songs about the Weaste and Eccles

Bayou and how hard it is being a truck driving man from Cheetham Hill.

Driving through Northumbria the other day I passed a town called Wide Open. I wonder how it got that name? Did somebody arrive in a place called Aullterfech one day, hear somebody say, 'This town's wide open,' and go home thinking that was its name so that when they asked him where he'd been said, 'This great little place called Wide Open'. But it has to be said that Northumbria takes the cream cracker when it comes to strange names. There is a village not a spit and a hop from Durham called Pity Me while, also in the same county, are the villages of Dragonville, No Place and Quaking Houses. Can you imagine being an estate agent in somewhere called Quaking Houses?

'Now don't worry, madam, it's only a name and as Shakespeare once said, "What's in a name? A rose by any other name would smell as sweet." '

'Aye bonny lad - well Shakespeare doesn't have tae live here and there'll be nae deposit till you change its name to Safezhouses.'

Driving round on your own doing my job does funny things to you. You sing at traffic lights and notice that people are staring at you, or you burst out laughing at something you hear on the radio. I always listen to Radio 4 and the other day I had to stop the car and get out and roll about on the grass verge laughing with my legs in the air. It was the day they announced that John Major's *Panorama* programme couldn't be broadcast in Scotland because it was too close to the Scottish elections. I could just imagine the tears and grief north of the border when they discovered they wouldn't be hearing England's most famous train spotter coming out with his usual drivel about 'feel good ... up turn just around the corner ... more money in real terms ... and safe in our hands.'

Hypnotising the Cat

'Morag lass, ma whole world's fallen apart the noo!! Ah cannae' see thon John Major on the telly this aye nicht.' Yes, I bet they were falling on their dirks with grief in Aulterfech that night.

Going back to Spring and Love and all that for a moment, there was something on television the other night about people's memories of their first loves, not first rudies you understand, this programme was about innocent first crushes. I remember with painful clarity falling in love when I was seven. I was staying at my Aunty Kitty's in Besses o'th'Barn which in those days was as close to 'out in the countryside' as I ever got. Across the avenue was a girl called Mavis and to me she was the most beautiful woman in the world. Close by Aunty Kitty's was Prestwich Clough which, before the M62 murdered it, was a lovely piece of quiet countryside. Mavis and the gang used to play there, and for the summer holidays I was an honorary member of that gang. As the days passed, my infatuation with Mavis deepened but the affection was not returned.

She was a mature eight-year-old beauty, impervious to the moon-faced adoration of a skinny and dreamy kid from four stations down the Bury-Manchester line. She politely refused my offers of cats' eyes I had prised out of the road and live newts I had collected from the ponds down in the Clough, though she was still woman enough to enjoy the adulation, and led me on with hints that while newts were not her particular favourites, tubes of Smarties might not be spurned. At night I would dream of rescuing her from wild Indians, the Emperor Ming and other baddies, thus earning her eternal love, but with the cold light of dawn I would be back in the real world of spurned newts.

When I finally saved up enough to buy Mavis a tube of Smarties it was too late, one of the Finegan twins had shown her his webbed toes and had won her love forever.

A tube of Smarties in the hands of a Crumpsall kid was no contender against something as interesting as webbed toes. Not for the last time I was outclassed and thwarted.

• •

Albert Tatlock's Illegitimate Son Marries Deirdre Barlow

For years I wanted to be in *Coronation Street*. You may laugh but for a start I wouldn't have far to go to work and I would certainly have no trouble with the accent, coming from '*Manchistor*' as I do. Since my good friend and fellow stand-up chuckle-merchant William Connolly once described me as 'runner-up in the Albert Tatlock look-alike competition' it has always seemed that a good way of getting into the programme might be for me to appear as Albert the Lollipop Man's long-lost illegitimate son. Once in, I take over Stan Ogden's old window cleaning round, cut my wrist on a broken pane of glass while cleaning Deirdre Barlow's windows and get invited in while she patches me up. One thing leads to another and before you know it ... well I'm sure some of you saw *The Postman Only Rings Twice*, this will be like that with Deirdre's scones all over the table, flour and pastry everywhere and me with one foot stuck in the bucket and the other stuck in the tip-up bin. I can see it now.

As you've probably worked out, it's a long time since I've watched *Coronation Street*. I tuned in the other night and was amazed. It took me quite a while to get back into it, working out who was who and where Ena Sharples and Albert Tatlock were, and why Elsie Tanner's American boyfriend wasn't in it any more - all that sort of thing. And it struck me that (apart from Sarah Lancaster as Raquel being the sexiest lady I have seen since I fell in love with Brigitte Bardot as a pimply newspaper boy of fourteen) there is something wrong with the programme. Wrong is perhaps too strong a word, unreal perhaps. Why are there no Pakistanis, Chinese, Gays, Irish, Crumblies, Poets, Catholic priests, banjo players or Nobby Carrs in the programme? Most of the people I know around town fall into that category and yet they never appear in the Street. I wish Granada would let me write the script; it would be much more like life as it is lived and less like *The Wizard of Oz* meets *Love on the Dole*.

Perhaps a small sample of the kind of thing I mean could influence the powers at Granada - you never know.

Scene 1. *The Rover's Return. Mysterious people whose lives we know nothing about are playing darts and drinking, flitting about in that shadow realm of Extra Land from which no one has ever returned. Jack Duckworth is super gluing his glasses to his nose. Raquel is staring into space communicating with the great soul of the universe. Bet Lynch is lying on the floor dead drunk, legs splayed and eyes akimbo. Enter Canon O' Connor.*

Canon O' Connor
Lord Save Us! Is it the last rites the poor woman is wanting?
Bet
'Eckerslike. Just give us another gin and throw another sailor under us.

Enter Nabbi Iqbal playing banjo and Henry Chow playing spoons.

Hypnotising the Cat

Nabbi

Sithee by 'eck, Bet, we can see all next weeks washin.'! Two pints Jack. What you 'avin' Father?

Canon O'Connor

A pint of Guinness and a dozen pickled eggs - the vestry wants fumigatin' - cockroaches, don't you know.

Enter Nobby Carr

Nobby

I've just been mugged by a Buddhist nun in the street. Can anybody lend me a couple of grand 'till Tuesday?

I await a phone call from the commissioning editor.

On a lighter note let me tell you a true story. My nephew Alex is five years old and we are trying to teach him manners - please and thank you, that sort of thing. We're an old fashioned sort of family that doesn't believe they should teach manners in school - school is where they should teach them to read and write not how to eat with a knife and fork or how to show respect to other people - teachers have a hard enough job of it as it is. Anyway, off the soapbox. The other day Alex ran into the house gibbering excitedly. 'Can I get a lolly out of the fridge, mummy? Can I? Can I? Can I get a lolly out of the fridge?'

We all looked at him stonily.

'What about the magic word?' expecting 'please' as a reply.

He thought for a moment then shouted 'Abracadabra - can I get a lolly out of the fridge now?'

• •

Hypnotising the Cat

A Letter From Belfast

I flew to Belfast earlier this week to appear on a television show. Jerry Anderson, who for a time had his own Radio Four series has a show called *Anderson on the Box* that is one of the most popular shows in Ireland. In theory I was supposed to be plugging a new book of short stories - *The Virgin of the Discos* - but in reality I just wanted to taste a pint of real Guinness again.

I had a pleasant flight over, sitting next to a Manchester surgeon who was on his way to perform keyhole surgery on three children in Belfast. We depressed ourselves talking about the NHS for a while and cursed Mrs. Bottomley roundly until people in seats about started looking at us. I often think at such times that if there was any truth in the old saw 'My ears are burning - somebody must be talking about me' then politicians would have to have a team of firemen permanently on call to throw buckets of water on their flaming lug-holes.

Tommy, the BBC driver, met me off the plane. Tommy has his own limo business and drives all the BBC guests around - we've known each other for years. He's about six foot four with steel-grey hair and a real Belfast sense of humour.

'How's the wee man?' he shouted as we threw the guitar and case into the boot. 'There's a boy wants your ortygraf on the way out.' And we stopped at the security checkpoint so I could give one of the flak-jacketed policemen my 'ortygraf'. I've been coming to Northern Ireland for more than twenty years and the sight of armed police, police stations with forty-foot fences and control towers and Saracens patrolling the streets with young English faces peering out along the barrels of their guns, doesn't give me the same tremors and worries that it used to. But I still get odd moments when the sphincter twitches and the reality of what the people here have to live through breaks in. One such moment happened on the way into town. I used always to stay at the Europa Hotel. It's right opposite the best Guinness well in Ireland - the Crown Bar - and is the most bombed hotel in the world outside Beirut. I noticed that Tommy was driving in a totally different direction.

'Am I not staying at the Europa?' I asked.

'Ah no,' says Tommy, 'the Europa got a wee touch.'

The 'wee touch' turned half the place to hardcore - such is the language of the Troubles. It was Tommy who drove me to the Europa a couple of years back when it was still all in one piece and explained that there was a lot of refurbishing going on . 'In fact,' he said, 'the next time you come, the front'll be round the side.' There is a truth and a logic in that sentence that you will only find in Ireland.

I had a radio show to do before lunch, with a lovely man, Colum Sands, whose brother Tommy wrote one of the best songs ever to come out of the troubles, 'Roses', a song based on a true story of two young men, one a Protestant, the other a Catholic. Close as any two brothers - they were both killed, within a few months of one another, by sectarian assassins for no reason other than that they were of the wrong religion. Ireland must be one of the few places in the world where people still write songs about real things. You can't imagine any of the turns in the charts in England singing a song about sectarian violence - or anything else that might strain the intelligence.

In the afternoon, with hours to kill before the show, I took a taxi to the Irish Cultural Centre on the Falls Road. I wanted some books on the Irish language, a subject I have been struggling with for years now. The black cabs that run along the Falls aren't taxis as we know them - they are like little black buses, people flag them down and crowd into them getting on and off just as you would a bus.

At the Cultural Centre I got talking to a group of

young people - all bright, friendly and thoughtful. There was a tiny girl amongst them - six years old or so with thick black hair and a grin wider than her face. I was wearing a jacket I was very proud of, a woollen sort of lumber jacket with an abstract pattern all in ochres and rusts. It's the kind of pattern and colour that would induce fits in a Rottweiler but I like it. I got it in the sale at Bilko's in the Royal Exchange. Forty quid it cost, reduced from ninety. The little girl looked at me for a moment.

'That jacket's yez are wearin's rubbish. Averybody's walkin round wearing 'em,' she said scornfully, and then went on crayoning. It turned out that a consignment of identical ninety pound jackets had fallen off a lorry and had hit the streets of Belfast at a fiver a time. On the way back to the studios I looked around. Even the tramps were wearing them. 'Out of the mouths of babes.'

Late that afternoon I did the sound-check and afterwards, waiting for the show to start, we somehow got talking about doctors and the things people say and Dave, one of the producers, gave me a piece of paper with some of the things Belfast doctors have heard over the last year or so from patients wanting to see them. Imagine the following being said in an Ulster accent:

'My wife can't breathe properly she has a weasel in her chest.
'Her head's that bad she can't get her tights on.'

'I've been bitten all over by midgets.'

'He has a rash on his legs and it's very itchy. It gets worse when he comes into heat.'

'I'd like an antibiotic for the wife.'
'Is she allergic to anything?'
'Yes, cats and paint.'

And my favourite ...

'He has terrible diarrhoea and I think it's coming through a hole in his teeth.'

Opening the show was a young Irish rock group with very strong folk influences called Goats Don't Shave. I first came across the name in Donegal last year. I was driving out of Glencolumbkille towards the mountains and, every so often at the side of the wild glen road, there were signs on posts hammered into the bog. 'Goats Don't Shave' was all the signs said. I wondered as I drove, was this some cryptic message to do with the IRA or the EEC and grants for razors for goats being slashed or something - you never know. On they went for miles following the road towards Killibegs. The matter was cleared up just before the town when the last sign said 'Goats Don't Shave - Killibegs Queens Hotel 19th August.

So when I met them I asked why the name Goats Don't Shave?

'We're from Donegal,' they said, 'there's an old farmer comes in our village pub. He goes on the tear for days on end and comes in to the pub looking wrecked, dirty and without a wash. "You're like an old mountainy goat," the landlord says. "Away and get a wash and a shave." "Goats don't shave," was all your man said. "Give us a pint and a Bush."' The band have a new record out soon. Check it out.

After the show it was across the road for a quick gargle in the Crown Bar which I forgot to mention is my Belfast office. The Crown is probably the most beautiful pub in the world. Its windows are Italian painted glass, its floor marble, its walls tiled and its bar all mahogany and brass. It is still gas-lit and there are drinking booths with doors and tiny windows where friends can meet for *'the craic'*. The barmen are fast and friendly and the food and drink are wonderful. The fact that it is a listed building owned by the National Trust makes it all the more bizarre.

Drinking late into the night with the cast and the crew and their relatives and friends, an elderly lady sat beside me and asked me,

'How do you like Ireland?'

'Love it.' I said.

'This would be the best wee country in the world if we could only get on with each other.'

She's so right. Ireland has some of the most wonderful landscape in Europe, it has a great musical tradition and the way the people use language, both English and Irish, is like nowhere else.

There was a wonderful postcard out a few years back showing a famous, anorexically-challenged, little known Harpurhey comedian called Bernard Manning stood at the microphone telling a gag. 'There was this thick Paddy ...' he begins and behind him on the wall is a simple list of names, Wilde, Shaw, Joyce, Yeats, O'Casey, Behan ...

On the way to the airport the next morning I told Tommy that I finally had the solution to the Northern Ireland problem.

'Think of what it's costing England to keep the army here and all the insurance and the rebuilding and the military hardware. Give everybody in the province a hundred thousand pounds on condition that they convert to Buddhism.'

'Ah, ' said Tommy, 'but you know what they'd say then - "Are ye a Catholic Buddhist or a Protestant Buddhist?"'

● ● ● ● ● ● ● ● ● ● ● ● ● ● ● ● ● ● ●

Tork Proper Ar Kid the Sperm Are Countin'

According to an article I read recently, dialect and accents are disappearing and we are all beginning to sound and speak alike. In fifty years time, avers the writer, people in the British Isles will all have a mid-Atlantic accent to sound like local radio station disc jockeys. I find that hard to believe. In spite of all the BBC and the rest have done to try and make us all sound like Trevor MacDonald, these islands are still rich in regional accents and dialects. Sit a true Cornishman down next to a Dundee fisherman and you'll be hard put to tell that they're from the same planet, never mind the same country.

Cornishman - Cor bugger moi tiddy oggie's all clappit.

Dundoonian - Ay ah'm aw drochit the noo and maw wee tattie scone's awa at the but and ben.

My mother, who had aspirations, spent years (well weeks at least, all right then, days) trying to get me to 'talk proper'. I remember it consisted mainly in me not saying 'kekkle, bokkle' and 'fink' for 'kettle, bottle' and think', and repeating over and over again the phrase - 'How now brown cow, sitting on the green green grass.' Since I had never seen a real cow and any green green grass was in the park and we were not allowed on it, the mantra was of no interest to me whatsoever and I soon tired of this drivel and within minutes of the lesson would be saying things like, 'As bin man bin mam?' meaning, 'Has the refuse collector collected the garbage mama?'

I was reminded of my Manchester patois the other day while sitting with Monsignor Nobby Carr in his office in the Midland Holiday Inn Crown Plaza Coffee Lounge. He'd just come back from a brief sojourn in Guernsey where he had been a guest of a well-known ex-Manchester night repairer of bathroom windows who has moved to Guernsey for the health of his wallet. A brief excerpt from Nobby's graphic travelogue follows ...

'That Guernsey - it's so upmarket that even the paraffins wear whistles. Emis! You guide down the frog and a paraffin with ream threads puts the arm on you - not for a bob for a mug of rosy and a slice of holy ghost - no danger - he wants a flin for a bottle of fizz, some strength bars and a swimmer.'

Roughly translated that reads:

'Guernsey is so posh that the tramps wear suits. I am not kidding! You walk down the street and a smartly dressed tramp accosts you asking not for a shilling for a cup of tea and a slice of toast but five pounds for a bottle of beer, chips and fish.'

I think it will be a while before we all sound like Jimmy Young or Julia Somerville.

I read in the paper this morning that, in the western world at least, the sperm count is going down year by year and that the Human Race could stand a chance of being cancelled by the end of the next century. Apparently, since records first began to be kept, the number of those little tadpoles they show you in the biology books in school are disappearing fast. Experts the world over seem to be blaming pollution from cars and industry and the rise in the general level of radiation from years of atomic emissions. I, on the other hand, blame tight underpants and television. Aha, I hear you mutter - another of Harding's lunatic theories to go in the bin with his other gems such as the one that goes - most Tory politicians are either mad, crooked or both, and his other one, that the Jehovah's Witnesses always call when you're having a crap. But not so hasty! Just consider this.

In the great days of the British Empire when chaps in baggy 'drawers cellular pairs one' went out to take the benefits of the English Public School system to the darkest corners of Africa, there were never any problems with the sperm count. Baggy drawers, according to British Army scientists, allow the breezes to circulate around the apparatus, thus keeping the gonads a degree or two lower in temperature than the rest of the body. Even the ancient Romans knew the importance of that. If you remember, all their soldiers went round in little leather skirts putting some Ancient Britons and Celts to the sword and getting the others pregnant, sometimes at the same time. In fact, as a form of contraception, Roman chaps would lower themselves into baths of hot water to kill some of the little taddies off before congress. It's a fact that ever since the jockey short took over from the baggy and flappy nethergarments of yesteryear there has been trouble in tadpole land.

'One moment,' I hear you ask, 'Where does television come in?' Well, to go back to history again, you may remember the pictures in your school books of primitive man stood in his furry shell suit looking down at the mammoths grazing on the plain, in his hand a long ash spear tipped at its end with half a brick, sharpened. His job basically was to run around chasing the dinner. It could take him all morning to kill a mammoth sometimes, and all that running would get his lymphatic system going and, at the same time, would swirl the primeval winds all about the old Palaeolithic family jewels.

What a wonder is modern man! Slumped in his armchair, the Chinese take-away steaming on his lap, staring for hours on end at the goggle box, his lymph gland as lively as a slug on a frosty morning, his gonads stewing like Mother Grogan's Irish stew, nicely trapped as they are in their cotton and nylon mixture cage and well insulated by the thick foam of the armchair seat. Had our ancestors sat there at the Dawn of Time, ensconced in an armchair made from a sabre-tooth tiger carcass, a stir-fry shredded mammoth with ginger and bean shoots festering on his lap, the human race wouldn't have made it to the Bronze Age. So if you wish to save the race, chaps, throw away your Y-fronts and zoom down to the ex-army stores and invest in several pairs of drawers cellular. Thus garbed, take yourself away to the local park and chase an imaginary mammoth for a couple of hours. Then if you've any strength left ... remember, you owe it to the human race.

Just a brief thought - who counts them anyway? The sperm I mean. Apart from the boredom, it must be a bit of a hit and miss affair. I can imagine them sat there, magnifying glass in one hand, hat-pin in the other, going, 'Two million seven hundred thousand six hundred and fifty-one, 'Two million seven hundred thousand six hundred and fifty-two, 'Two million seven hundred thousand six hundred and fifty-three'... The door opens and a junior comes into the lab. 'The winning raffle ticket numbers are six hundred and twenty-two, one hundred and twelve and nine hundred and ninety-six'. The door closes, the magnifying glass goes back up again and a desperate voice intones, 'One, two, three - that's a dead 'un - four, five six - the tail's fell off that one ... '

● ●

Cupla Focal Gaelge - a letter from Donegal

I'm off to Sligo in a couple of days to climb Benbulbin and Knocknaree but first I'm spending a week in Glencolumbkille, County Donegal, at an Irish language school. One of my great ambitions is to get enough Irish under my belt to be able to hold a basic conversation with native speakers. It hasn't happened yet and like the Greek and Urdu I learned a few years back it just means that I can confuse yet another set of people in something that sounds like their own language but isn't. I've tried learning from tapes and books but it hasn't worked all that well. The do-it-yourself course I've been working from goes from 'Hello. The weather today is beautiful, thanks be to God', to 'Where is the donkey that ate the children's homework?' in three pages. Not a great deal of use during ordinary chat, I would have thought.

One time a couple of years back or so while cycling along a country road in the *Coolea Gaeltacht* (Irish-speaking area) of County Cork, I came across two old men who were stacking turf at the side of the road. Ah, I thought, just the very opportunity to practise my *cupla focal Gaelge* (couple of words of Irish). I ripped into them with some of my very best page one. They stared at me open-mouthed for a moment, then one of them crossed himself and began fumbling for his rosary, convinced that I was either possessed by the devil or was speaking in tongues, courtesy of the Holy Ghost. After a couple of minutes of one-way conversation about the weather, I ran off page two on to page three and asked them where the donkey was that had ate the children's homework, at which point they fled.

It was in County Cork that I first met Johnny Crowley

of Bantry, a lovely man and one of the best storytellers I have met. It was John who pointed out a man to me in a little pub in Cork some years back saying:

'D'you see your man over there?'

'I do,' says I, looking at a tall thin man in an old gaberdine raincoat.

'Well, he's a fine pianist and when the filums first came to Bantry he was asked to play the piano for them. They were the silent filums and they had to have music with them.

"How do I do that?" asks your man.

"Well," says the manager, "You just watch the screen and play any tune at all that suits the pictures."

'Well, the first filum was the *Life of Christ*. And when Our Lord was walking on the water your man played "Over the Waves" and there was a few titters at that. When He was carrying the cross he played "The Rocky Road to Dublin" and there was a few more titters. But what really brought the house down was when He was raising Lazarus from the dead and your man played "Come back Paddy Reilly to Ballinjamesduff". '

I've a suspicion that story is true because several other people told me the same tale, all about the same man. But if it isn't true then isn't it enough that it's a good story? And as someone once said, 'Never let the truth get in the way of a good tale.'

The language course was an intensive week in which Irish was the only language spoken and Guinness was the only beverage drunk. The *craic* (fun) was ninety (excellent) and the music in the little pubs in the village was world-class. It never ceases to please me that in the heart of some of the poorest land in western Europe where people have scraped a bare living from bog and rocky mountain there beat some of the biggest hearts in the world and there is made some of the great music of the world. In Glencolumbkille this week I sat in a pub with one of the great musicians of western Europe, a Donegal farmer called James Byrne. He has farmers' hands, great strong thick fingers used to lifting and digging and hauling and birthing lambs, yet from those same hands came some of the sweetest airs and wildest tunes I've ever heard.

'Your hearts are like your mountains
In the homes of Donegal', runs the old song and it's true. I remember once walking along the *bohareens* (little roads) of the Bluestack Mountains with a man called Paddy Campbell, a small man with a big heart and a shiny face like a polished apple. It took us almost a whole day to walk something like five miles because so many people called us into their homes. I met an old man called Jimmy McCrory who lived in a thatched cottage all alone. A great 'rambling man', he would spend the long winter evenings walking from house to house sitting and talking and singing the odd song. I met a woman who had spent thirty odd years working as a clippie on the trams and buses of Glasgow but had come home to retire. And there were so many more. All of them shouted us in and each time the kettle went on and a plate of soda bread and butter was put on the table. By the end of the afternoon I had more than a gallon of tea inside me and it was hard to walk because it was all sloshing about. I was like a hot-water bottle on legs.

I didn't get much chance for walking in Donegal this time because I was supposed to be in school. I did pinch a couple of hours one evening, though, to climb up to the old martello tower that stands on the sea cliffs above the glen. It was a magic evening with the sun in the west and tiny clouds crawling in from the Atlantic Ocean across a blue sky. I did my climb and was walking back along a muddy *bohareen* when I came across a little girl crying.

'What's the matter?' I asked.

'The donkey has ate my homework' she said.

I knew it would come in handy one day.

A Letter From Sligo

This could be one of those apocryphal tales or it might not - you never know. A story currently going the rounds in Ireland concerns a recent court case in Cork involving a German sailor who came into Cork on a ship, got drunk and assaulted a policeman. Seemingly he had no English at all so when he was up before the beak the next morning, he couldn't even give his name. 'Does anybody in this court speak German?' asked the Judge.

'I do your honour,' cried a little Corkman from the gallery.

'Come down here and translate. First of all ask him his name,' says the Judge.

The little Corkman strides up to the hapless sailor and shouts in best British film-industry German, 'Vat iz your name?' The little Corkman was given thirty days for contempt. I don't know what happened to the sailor.

Sligo, where I am now, is a magical place. I have to be careful when I'm writing about Ireland because I'm definitely a fan and I would always rather talk about the positive rather than the negative sides of the country. I don't want to give you the impression that the place is stuffed full of old men on donkey carts going, 'Top of the morning to yez, sor!' and other such rubbish. Ireland is a romantic country with a beautiful landscape and a wonderful culture. It is also part of modern Europe and suffers from many of the ills of its neighbours including pollution, inappropriate development and a fair smattering of 'cute hoor' politicians. But the positive far outweighs the negative, and Sligo, as I said, is a magical place. When you walk in the hills and lakeside forests of Sligo you're walking on five thousand years of Irish mythology and through the words of one of the greatest poets that ever graced the

Hypnotising the Cat

English language - W.B. Yeats. I know he had his problems, was an out-and-out bar-steward to his wife and probably wouldn't at all be the kind of bloke I'd like to have a jar with, but some of his poetry still can make the hair stand on the back of my neck. I know that there is nothing modern about his stuff and that he is often overblown and romantic to the point of vanishing up his own *bohareen* but still there is never any doubt but that he's writing poetry as against prose stuck in broken lines:

I will arise and go now, and go to Innisfree,
And a small cabin build there, of clay and wattles made:
Nine bean rows will I have there and a hive for the honey-bee
And live alone in the bee-loud glade.

I stood this morning on the shores of Lough Gill and looked across to Innisfree, the lake as still as lead and the small island shining in the early sun. I could understand then how Yeats wrote that poem in the fogs of London, wishing himself back amongst the hills he loved. Further along the lakeshore is the great rock of Dooney where the fiddler in another of Yeats's poems came from. The fiddler has a brother and a cousin who are priests. But:

When we come to the end of time
To Peter sitting in state,
He will smile at the three old spirits,
But call me first through the gate

For the good are always the merry
Save by an evil chance,
And the merry love the fiddle,
And the merry love to dance ...

Hypnotising the Cat

Yeats is buried under Benbulbin a massive mountain with formidable cliffs. From a distance it looks like a great stone ship that has run aground above the coastal plains of Sligo. I climbed it yesterday scrambling up a gully on to its wild rim. Far below I could see the tiny churchyard at Drumcliffe where Yeats is buried. On his tombstone are the cryptic words:

Cast a cold eye
On life, on death
Horseman, pass by

The last lines of his last poem.

I heard another lovely Cork story this week. During the troubles of the early quarter of this century the Black and Tans were zooming round the Cork countryside in armoured lorries while the IRA had nothing but bicycles and donkeys. Now Henry Ford had just opened his first European car-plant in Cork and it was stuffed full of lorries. In came some of the boys in their belted raincoats and Sam Brownes to hold up the manager and requisition some vehicles for the cause. The manager, being a wily Kerryman said:

'These lorries are the property of a citizen of the United States of America and since this country is not at war with America you can't have them.'

'Give me a piece of paper,' said the IRA commander to his second in command. He hurriedly scribbled a note. It read, 'I hereby solemnly declare that as of this moment this country is at war with the United States of America'.

'Now,' says the commander, 'Give us those bloody lorries.'

I was in Mayo last week doing a bit of this and that but none of the other, and came across some very interesting pieces of information while I was helping to reduce Ireland's Guinness Mountain. There I was, sat with my pint of Black Mischief and my plate of bacon and cabbage in the bar in Westport where I was mis-spending some of my middle years when I noticed that the beer mats in the bar had printed on them interesting facts about Irish saints, sponsored I suppose by Opus Dei. My Guinness went flat and my dinner went cold as I perused the beer mats in amazement. Did you know for example that St Brigid is the patron saint of milkmen or that St Cathal is the patron saint of hernia sufferers? Those of you who sleepwalk are looked after by St Dympna while St Fiacre takes care of taxi-drivers and anybody with haemorrhoids. And mock ye not, for a certain English king called Henry laid waste the chapel of St Fiacre only to die a year later on the feast day of St Fiacre of septic haemorrhoids.

It was while I was in Mayo that two momentous events took place, one was the IRA cease-fire, the other was Matchmaker's Week in Lisdoonvarna. I am not going to be facetious or flip about the cease-fire; like many people, I find the subject of the Troubles too complex and tragic to offer any simple or glib solutions. I know where my sympathies lie but I also know that there are many dimensions that have to be explored and taken into consideration and that it won't all suddenly come right overnight. Like many people, too, I just hope and pray that the beautiful island and the people of that island will soon find a kind of peace and harmony. God alone knows, they need it after all these years.

The Matchmaker's Week, though, is another thing entirely. For aeons bachelor farmers have been coming to Lisdoonvarna, just to the north of the great limestone barrens of the Burren in County Clare, at this time of the year, just after the hay-making and just before the tupping time. They came looking for wives, and, since they were often shy old mountainy men, there soon sprung up a whole body of professional matchmakers who would ask them what kind of a wife they were looking for. A widow? Own teeth? Young? Old? Anything with a pulse? With a little bit of land?

Of course they asked the same thing of the women too and then tried to match them up. It was an early form of Guinness-powered computer dating. It still goes on to some extent though much of it has been turned into an excuse for a party now. Interestingly, in the last few years quite a few American women have been coming to the Matchmaker's Week. God knows how they would handle some of the mountain men I know. My dear friend Johnny Crowley was telling me about one matchmaker who pointed out one lady to a prospective groom and said, 'She has the grass of six cows and the whole of Bantry Bay', meaning that she had land enough for six cows and the right to fish in the bay. There is a music in much Irish speech that reflects the great beauty of the original Gaelic language. Talking to a gravedigger who was digging a grave in Kilfenora, County Clare a couple of weeks back, and expecting him at any moment to pull up a skull and exclaim, 'Alas poor Paidric, I knew him well', I said, 'The Matchmakers are up at Lisdoonvarna, do you not fancy travelling up there and finding yourself a nice woman?'. He leant on his shovel and looked up at me.

'Sure and why should I go all the way up there and pay a man to find me an ugly one when I can stay down here in Kilfenora and find a good-looking one for meself?'

One of the best storytellers I ever met lived in Clare. His name was Michael Vaughan and he ran the Aberdeen Arms Hotel in Lahinch. A short example of Michael's style follows, though I could never capture that soft Clare accent or the way he looked into the distance when he was telling a story as though being guided by something su- pernatural, his face as straight as a pan while he told the wildest and most comical stories, all of which, of course,were true.

'I was in the lounge one morning,' he told me once, 'when this big Yank who was staying here for the golf came in. He was in a heck of a fluster so I sat him down and made him a cup of tea. "Now what's your problem," I says to him? "This country is driving me crazy," he says, "I've been trying to find a telex machine round here but they ain't got one and I need to telex my broker in LA. I went down to the post office and there was a line a mile long because somebody was buying a dog licence and couldn't remember what kind of dog it was he wanted the licence for and while he was stood there somebody said sure and isn't the dog outside and the guy went out to take a look at it and came back and said it was part mongrel, part mixed and the guy gave him the licence. Then there was a godawful bang and somebody came in and said the dog had just been run over and killed. And it had. So this guy asked for his money back but the post office clerk said that the licence had been issued and there was no way he was going to get his money back. Then this guy called the clerk some names and a row started up and went on for half an hour. Nobody seemed bothered. The line just stood there watching. No sense of hurry at all. This place is worse than Mexico. Tell me something Michael," he says to me. "Do the Irish have a word in the Gaelic that is like mañana?" Well, I thought for a minute and said "We do, but it doesn't have quite the same sense of urgency." '

• •

Bugs Bunny in 'There's No Bizniz Like Agro Bizniz'

Errnnn. What's up Doc?' exclaimed Bugs Bunny, the Pesky Wabbit, gnawing on his twenty-fifth carrot that day.

'Well,' said the Doc. 'I've had a good look at you and it seems that the reason you have been getting dizzy and falling over and seeing lots of little fat men with guns that aren't really there is carrots.'

'Cawwots!!! Gnick! Gnick! Gnick! Whaddya mean Cawwots? Cawwots is good fer wabbits! Cawwots help you see in the dark and give you curly fur! Cawwots makes a wabbit big and stwong! That's what every mummy wabbit tells her baby wabbits.'

'Not these carrots,' the doctor said sadly. 'These carrots have been dosed with organo-phosphate.'

'Organy pwostate!' Bugs Bunny spat out a lump of carrot and threw the rest into the doctor's waste bin. 'Organy pwostate! What the Watership Down is organy pwostate when it's at home?'

'It's one of the components of nerve gas. It's the kind of thing that Saddam Hussein was stockpiling in the Gulf War and it's been used on all those clean and perfect carrots that you see in the supermarkets. The ones that are all the same size. The ones we are told that the housewife wants, the carrots you've been eating for the last ten years.'

Bugs Bunny clutched his heart and sank back in the chair.

'So de fawmers have been using noive gas on de poor innocent cawwots. Was these cawwots a thweat to society? Was these cawwots Awab cawwots? Was these cawwots after our oil?'

'Well, not exactly, it's a little more complex than that. You see years ago carrots came in all sorts of shapes and sizes, big, small, lumpy, two-tailed and hairy and they were dirty and people had to wash them. In those days the farmers just fed them soot and manure and let nature do the rest. Then the scientists and the farmers decided that the way to sell more carrots was to make them all the same size so they used nitrates on them and grew them all very close together. And to stop flies laying eggs on them and causing disease they had to spray them with organo-phosphates. Now the Ministry of Agriculture has told us that we have to top and tail and peel all carrots because they've absorbed the nerve gas.'

'But the noive gas will go in troo de leaves!' said the Pesky Wabbit. 'It'll be insoide de cawwot so what's de good of peelin' it? Aaargh I've been poisoned by the Agro Chemical Industwy!!!' He reeled back clutching his throat. 'Where can I buy orgasmic cawwots? A wabbit's got to eat cawwots.'

'You can get organic carrots from a little farm I know in Cumbria, just south-west of Sellafield. You can tell that they help you to see because they glow in the dark. They're perfectly good for you, a bit of radiation never hurt anybody. Ask the people of Hiroshima.'

There was a sudden high-pitched scream and then a crash as Bugs Bunny leaped through the window, leaving a rabbit-shaped hole in the glass. The doctor looked through the window, but sadly, the Pesky Wabbit was not standing on thin air, and no parachute had suddenly appeared from out of fat air, as in most of his best films. Bugs had fallen thirty floors and was now rabbit jam on the pavement. There was a knock at the door. The nurse entered. 'It's Peter Rabbit and Mr. Macgregor,' she said. 'Peter Rabbit keeps falling over and Mr. Macgregor has trouble breathing which he thinks may be to do with sheep dip.'
There was a sudden high-pitched scream and then a crash

as the doctor leaped through the window, leaving a doctor-shaped hole in the glass.

The nurse looked in the waste bin. 'Ah,' she said, 'just as I thought - he's been at the carrots again.'

So, fifty years ago the Allied troops met in Berlin and the mad unitesticulate painter and decorator and his girlfriend met their end in the Bunker. It all seems like another world now - which of course it was - Anderson Shelters, rationing, stirrup pumps and women covering their legs with gravy browning and drawing seams down the back to look like stockings. Family legend has it that my grandmother refused to come out of the air-raid shelter because she didn't trust the Germans and thought they were only kidding.

'But Mr. Churchill has told us that the war's over and the Germans have surrendered.'

'Churchill is it?' my gran spluttered in her Dublin accent. 'I knew him when he was a window cleaner and hadn't a ha'penny to scratch his backside with. He never did the corners properly and was always knocking on the door asking for more hot water!'

It was no use telling her that Frank Churchill the window cleaner, who was now digging latrine trenches in the Pioneer Corps at Lytham St Anne's, was nothing to do with the fat man with the cigar who was famous for asking everybody else for their blood, sweat and tears while he sat in his armchair swigging brandy and smoking cigars and having nightmares about black dogs.

'Ah,' I hear you say, 'but Churchill was a great statesman - without him we would have lost the war.' Well I would argue about that - but can I also remind you that he was a politician and it was politicians that got us all into the mess in the first place. Perhaps they eat too many cawwots.

Because something is certainly up, Doc.

Burglars' Question Time

With the removal of Gardeners' 'Question Time from BBC Radio 4 a hole could possibly be created in the programming schedule that needs filling quickly if audiences are not all to secede to Classic FM. Any BBC executives that read this column please note that the following idea is copyright M. Harding 1995 but is up for grabs for lots of lolly. Based on the idea that after gardening and fishing, burglary must take a close third place, in terms of numbers of people involved in the hobby, I present:

Burglar's Question Time

In the chair - 'Fingers' Larsen, Strangeways and the Scrubs.
The Panel - Dr Stefan Knockoffsky, Walton and Parkhurst, Fred Loot, Strangeways and Durham and 'Jemmy' Entwhistle, Risley, Hull, Peterhead and Armley.

Fingers
Our programme today comes from Dartmoor. The soil is thin and peaty and there's miles of it. Any lag going over the wall faces the twin prospects of frostbite and the Black Beast of Dartmoor (which, by the way, is believed to be an escaped panther) - both the frostbite and the Black Beast go for anything dangling, so people round here tend to make sure that they are well lagged - if you'll pardon the pun. Our first question is from Albert 'the Jewels' Jones - twelve years, aggravated burglary.

Albert
I've noticed that during the winter months the locks on conservatory doors tend to get frozen up which makes

them hard to force. Can the panel suggest anything whereby I can prevent frozen fingers, split nails and a lot of noise?

Fingers
Frozen locks - any ideas? Stefan.

Stefan
A lot of the old boys used to take cotton waste and a little tin of lighter fuel with them - they'd stuff the waste in the keyhole after soakin' it wiv petrol then put a glim to it. That used to thaw out the lock quite well, although one or two of them got too keen with the petrol and burnt down the houses they were tryin' to burgle. Ha Ha Ha (laughter all round). No, to be serious - nowadays there is so much good stuff on the market you are spoilt for choice. A simple can of windscreen de-icer will do the job in a jiffy. It's quiet and clean and you can also use it for the windscreen of the getaway car.

Fred
This newfangled stuff is all well and good, but you know I think you'll go a long way to beat my old dad's method. You just get your lips round it and blow.

Stefan
And what about if yer lips get froze to the keyhole? There you are stuck - in come the bogies - Nick Nick - You're done my son!

Fred
Ah but you see - the real burglar who knew what he was doing wouldn't apply his lips to the bare metal - he'd put a handkerchief over the metal first and blow through that.

Hypnotising the Cat

Fingers
He's got you there Stefan! Jemmy, have you any ideas on frozen locks?

Jemmy
Ten seconds with one of them little gas cylinder blow lamps and if that doesn't work - kick the bleedin' door in, grab the video and leg it.

Fingers
And you find this has worked for you?

Jemmy
Free times out of four it did. The fourf I was just unlucky. Fell over the dustbin - did me 'ead in. Ner ner ner ner - blue light, bracelets and a bed for the night courtesy of Her Majesty - God Bless Her.

Fingers
Our next question is from Everest John from Birmingham - doing a straight eight for stealing John Major's O Level results. It was one for stealin' em and seven for sellin' em to the *Daily Mirror*. Everest is a Cat burglar -known round his turf as the Chris Bonnington of the North face of Suburbia. Everest, your question is about fencing I believe.

Everest
Yer. Does the panel know of any good fences where I can get rid of tasty stuff like diaries, address books and photographs of cabinet ministers wiv naked women sittin' on their knees undoin' their ties? Or am I better off plantin' them and waitin' until they start offerin' buy back money?

Hypnotising the Cat

___

Fingers

Stefan?

Stefan

It's a toss-up really. I'd plant them and wait - you never know. Once it gets a bit hot you'll get a better return for your trouble.

Fingers

Jemmy?

Jemmy

To me it depends on the variety of the subject - if it's pansies yer talkin' about - Bertie Wooftahs an that - then the *Telegraph* always likes a bit of that. Otherwise for general stuff I think you should get yourself a good agent.

Fingers

Now that's a thought Fred. What would you call a good agent?

Fred

Well as a starter - as a general rule - I always say nine parts Barabas to one part crocodile is about right.

Fingers

Well, that's all we've time for this week. Next week's programme comes from Strangeways etc. etc. etc.

• •

The Revenge of The Spaghetti House Mob

From time to time I am forced to be away from my day job as a hack for the Manchester Evening News. When that happens other people do my column. On this occasion it was Damon Runyan writing, from beyond the grave, with the help of Doris Stokes and a ouija board. Canon O'Connor was on hand with a fire extinguisher full of holy water in case any bad spirits tried to cross from the other side.

So I am sat in my favourite speakeasy, the Golden Rivet, with Harry the Horse, Lou the Nose and Mo the Lawn when Norman the Carr makes an entrance. He gives us all greetings as is his custom and then sits down. But I notice that more than somewhat his face looks as though he has lost a pound and found a shilling so I say to him, 'Welcome, old timer. Why is the brow so wrinkled, the eyes so clouded and the hands so shaky?'

'Ah,' he sighs. 'It is all on account of the fact that there are certain persons in this burgh that can be very injurious to a citizen's health and such persons are seeking out yours truly over a small misunderstanding regarding a certain business deal.'

Now it is a known fact that while he never does anything illegal, Norman the Carr sails close to several winds and is what is known as a ducker and diver among the citizens of this parish. He stares at the cup of coffee that is growing cold in front of him, fills his pocket with the free nuts and packets of sweeteners and sighs again.

'In fact things are so bad that I am seriously thinking of going underground.'

Hypnotising the Cat

'They are closing all the mines down,' says Mo the Lawn, who is a gladiolus short of a flower show on account of having been run over by a truck driven by Legs Akimbo while working as a hit man for the Eccles Mob.

'The underground I am thinking of is somewhere like Malta or Abyssinia or the South Sea Islands. In fact, had I the mazooma to facilitate such a project I would be on Concorde now with nothing but a toothbrush and a clean change of wallets.'

'Is the story one that can be told or will we all have to wait until the coroner's inquest?' asks Harry the Horse, who is not known for his diplomacy.

'It is a story you will hear soon enough in any case,' says Norman. 'So I will tell you now so that you get it from the donkey's muzzle.

'I am sitting in the Pig and Ballbearing a few days back minding some business when Antonio the Italian barber makes an entrance. He knows that I do the occasional line in cheeky videos and is desirous of purchasing same for a party certain male members of the Spaghetti Shovellers Union are having while their wives are on a cheap shopping weekend to London. Now as you know I have no video player myself so do not know what is on these particular goods I deal in. "Here you are," I say to him, handing him a tape I have bought that morning in good faith. "Poolside Frolics" it said on the label and never was an honest ducking and diving citizen so misled than on that occasion.

'I hear later that Antonio phones up the men and boys who work in the various Spaghetti Joints, Coiffure Parlours and Hokey Pokey Penny A Lick establishments in this burgh and on Saturday last, after their work is done, they all go to Antonio's. A few bottles of wine, a nice Tuscan meal later, they all sit back to watch "Poolside Frolics". The titles roll and then a young lady with a chest that would have graced pages 3, 4 and 5 of the *Sun*, wearing only the skimpiest of bathing suits, comes into the picture. There is heavy breathing amongst the assembled multitude and the canary collapses in his cage and dies from all the exhaled garlic fumes. The young lady smiles to camera. There are groans and more heavy breathing because she is a very fetching young lady and would certainly have a hard time of it as a nun. Then the same young lady bends down and picks up a hoop and holds it over the pool. Suddenly a dolphin jumps through it and for the next hour and a half several young ladies walk round the pool in skimpy clothing as dolphins balance balls on their snouts and walk on the water on their tails. Then the credits roll and thirty-four Italian chefs, barbers and waiters are out on the streets looking for yours truly with homicide in their hearts. And it is not my fault because I am buying "Poolside Frolics" in good faith. Ah, woe is me - why was I ever born to die ignobly on the end of a Milanese barber's styling comb?'

'Ah but,' said Lou the Nose, who considers himself something of an advocate and legal eagle, 'It is beholden to every retailer to check the quality of goods he is offering for sale.'

'Shut your cake-hole before I fill it with this ashtray,' said Norman the Carr mournfully. 'I have nothing to look forward to but exile.'

'Well, look on the bright side,' says Mo the Lawn. 'You can take turns with Lord Lucan and Salman Rushdie to ride Shergar.'

● ●

A Touch of the Jane Austens

*A*nother time I was on holiday my job was done for me by Jane Austen, with the help of course of a ouija board and Doris Stokes.

It is a truth universally acknowledged that a single man in possession of a good fortune must be in want of a wife and when Mr. Brook Contradiction took the tenancy of Thirteen Thatcher Crescent in the town of ... in the county of ... the hearts of elderly matron and eligible young lady alike were fired with both curiosity and excitement.

'La Ma!' shrilled Tracey Bennet to her mother one morning as she was cleaning one of the stolen videos her brother Jason had brought home from his night job as a repairer of bathroom windows. 'Me n' Shaz saw that new bloke that's moved into number thirteen in the offy! 'Ee's a drink on a stick int 'ee Shaz?'

'Yer,' said Sharon from her prone position on the settee where she was ensconced perusing *Hello!* magazine, looking for words of less than six letters and two syllables, such as 'Queen' and 'Royal' and 'film star' and 'money'. Fortunately for her the magazine contained little else, though she did have occasional trouble with such long words as 'Millionaire', 'Princess' and 'paparazzi'.

'Wot I fink is that we should 'ave a party an invite 'im Mam.'

'Wot a brill idea our Trace!' mumbled Sharon over the buzzing of her Ladyshave. 'We can get some nibbles and drinks in. Our Jase can gerrum nicked by that bloke he knows at the club.'

And so invitations were printed and duly sent to announce to Mr. Brook Contradiction and the better families in Thatcher Crescent that Mr. and Mrs. Kenny Bennet of the same street were giving a party to which they were all invited RSVP. Eagerly the daughters of the Bennet household waited for the replies to flop through the letterbox and, one by one, cards and notes arrived back until all, including the new tenant at number thirteen, had accepted the invitation.

For days Bennet Hall was a flurry of cleaning and tidying.

'Shift them bleedin' tights of yours off that chair our Trace. You're a right mucky cow you are. What are people goin' to fink if you've got half your undies draped all over the shop?'

'People can fink wot they like,' responded Tracey. 'And you can talk! I found one of your false eyelashes stuck to the lavvy pan this mornin'. I nearly wet meself, I thought it was a spider.'

'It must 'ave flew off when I was bein' sick last night. I fink somethin' upset me.'

'Probably that twenty-second glass of cider and black-currant that bloke with the BMW convertible bought you in the Atlas Bar.'

'Shurrit yew,' retorted Sharon. 'Yer only jealous 'cos you fancied 'im yerself an' ended up shaggin' that one-armed winder cleaner wiv the blue metallic Cinquecento!'

And so the gentle friendly badinage continued until on the day of the party, after all three of the ladies of the household had visited the coiffurier and the sun bed and all provisions had been made, the guests began to arrive.

Sharon and Tracey awaited the entrance of Mr. Contradiction with great, though disguised, eagerness and when at last he swept through the door, an observant bystander, had he been close by the tropical fish tank, would have perceived more than a faint flush upon their cheeks and bosoms.

He behaved very much as a gentleman should, paying equal attention to both daughters and being civil and courteous to Mrs. Bennet and Mr. Bennet in even quantities, so that when all four retired to the kitchen to bring out the sausage rolls and the egg and mayonnaise baps, they passed a hurried verdict on the new arrival in their social circle.

'He fills his trousers well is all I can say,' said Mrs. Bennet.

'In't 'ee good lookin' mam?' replied Tracey.

''Ee's too much meat for you our Trace.' squealed Sharon with mischief in her voice.

'I think 'ee's a bit of a Bertie Wooftah meself. Punt é Mes and soda 'ee asked for. That's a tart's drink, that is.' said Mr. Bennet, replenishing the dry roasted peanuts.

'No, you can 'ave that when yer stomach's off,' replied Mrs. Bennet,'Perhaps 'ee's been down Rusholme and got a touch of Gandhi's Revenge.'

For the rest of the evening Mr. Contradiction circled the room dancing at one moment with Tracey, the next with Sharon and, as becomes a gentleman of his standing, never for one moment neglecting Mrs. Bennet.

Still there are ripples in the tides and times of Men (and Women!) that none of us, lest we have the powers of divination, may foresee. And so it was that scarcely six months after, *Hello!* magazine, on its problem page, printed the following missive:

Dear Gabby,
A bit back we had a party at our house because me and my sister fancied this bloke. He seemed all right and in fact even me mam fancied him. But we now learn that he is gay and has run off with our Dad who has decided he is gay too and they are running a chip shop in Poulton le Fylde. Please advise.
Yours
Tracey and Sharon Bennet (and Mam)

● ● ● ● ● ● ● ● ● ● ● ● ● ● ● ● ● ● ● ●

The Grabbits of Grabbit Hall

*L*ast year was Manchester's turn to wear the City of Drama
T-shirt and at the time it seemed only natural that I, as
the author of several plays, one of which had run for some
time in the West End (well, it didn't run, it sort of stumbled)
thought I ought to get my two pennorth in. Any budding
playwrights should know that you never send a whole play in for
consideration, just a résumé of the plot and a couple of scenes to
give the artistic director an idea of what you're trying to do. I
offer as an example my own humble submission, a drama written
after the fashion of those other great dynastic epics such as The
Forsyth Saga *and* Noggin the Nog.

THE GRABBITS OF GRABBIT HALL

BY

M. HARDING GENT.

Act 1
Scene 1
*The drawing room of the Grabbits' mansion. Through a window
we see a millscape, though almost all the mills are now Texas
Home Stores, B&Qs or Cannon and Ball Cinemas. It is dusk on
Christmas Eve, the maid is lighting the candles and little Evie
is playing selections from Iron Maiden, Take That and Max
Bygraves on the piano.*

Mr. Grabbit

By 'eck Evie when tha rattles yon ivories that chuffs me
reet oop, ah get fair thraipsed and clagwarched tha knows.
Eee! all them lessons wi yon Clayderman feller were brass
well spent. Eh up sithee mother!! Yon ferret's chewin'
t'wire on t' video - purr it wi thi clog.

Hypnotising the Cat

Mrs. Grabbit

Lawks a mussy father!! That damn ferret'll eat owt. It ate one of t' worker's bairns last week, it cost seventy-five pee to keep her quiet.

Mr. Grabbit

Tha shouldn't let me best ferret eat muck like that! Worker's bairns! They're not even washed! It might dee, tha gurt silly wazzock! (*He fetches her a right wallop and she falls down in a swoon.*)

Evie

Oh father, such language! - and anyway it were only a small babby - it wouldn't have choked it.

Mr. Grabbit

(*In a huff, turning to poke the gas-log effect fire with a poker-effect poker*) Well, I just wish you'd take better care, that's all.

(*Enter Ralf Grabbit, sneering, hand-wringing, moustàchioed, ne'er-do-well eldest son of the Grabbit clan.*)

Ralf

(*Ingratiatingly*) Good evening father, mother, Evie.

Mr. Grabbit

Oh!! So ye've decided to come home have you? By - tha's getten a brass neck my lad! I gave thee five pounds to go to t'corner shop for a bag of Uncle Joe's Mint Balls six weeks ago and tha's only just come back now. Where are they, any road up sithee by 'eck?

Hypnotising the Cat

Ralf

I et 'em father.

Mr. Grabbit

(*Furious*) Et em! Et 'em! To eat one Uncle Joe's is a damn cheek, to eat the whole bloody bag is nothing short of a left wing statement against international capital!! You've got a cheek you 'ave! I suppose you've been out gettin' all t' lasses in Inkerman Street in t' family way again.

Ralf

And Sebastapol Terrace - apart from them two in th' end house.

Mr. Grabbit

You did right lad - them at the end 'ouse are probably lesbians anyway.

Evie

Father!!

Mr. Grabbit

They wear flat shoes, vote Labour and won't shag our Ralf. In my book that makes 'em Lesbians.

Mrs. Grabbit

(*As Evie is bandaging her head*) Oh our Ralf! Whatever will your fiancée, Miss Evelyn Crump, have to say!

Ralf

She's in t' family way too, mother.

Hypnotising the Cat

Evie

Our Ralf, you're nothing but a common tom cat!

Ralf

Well, if it's good enough for t'government - it's good enough for me.

(There is a knock at the door and Tom Catshit falls in. He is exhausted. His face is blackened and there are obvious scorch marks on his ragged clothing.)

Tom

There's trouble at t' mill maister.

Mr. Grabbit

Nay Tom! Men aren't out on strike for food again are they?

Tom

No sir - they love starvin' - honest they do. They 'ave starving competitions to see who can get thinnest soonest. It's not that.

Mr. Grabbit

What is it then?

Tom

One of the lepers 'as self-combustulated in t'gusset testin' shed. Mrs. Groggins is dead and little Elsie Sputum will never walk again.

Mrs. Grabbit

She 'ad rickets anyway. It's a blessing. I used to hate seeing her pass the house gates swinging from side to side like that. Sometimes the mobilely challenged can be so unsightly.

Mr. Grabbit
(Thinking) Elsie Groggins dead! *(Aside)* So she takes the secret of our mucky weekend in Morecambe with her to the grave! *(Out loud)* Elsie Groggins - she's been with me twenty-five years! Think of t'redundancy brass I'll save! Think of all t'insurance money!

Ralf
(White-faced, having taken a sheaf of papers from a drawer which he is holding in his hand) Father, I've checked the small print on the policy - we're not insured for exploding lepers!

Mr. Grabbit
Not insured! Sithee by 'eck we're ruined!! Blast that silver-tongued devil from the Pru!!

(Mrs. Grabbit and Evie swoon to the floor with the vapours. The two men stare glumly into the gas-log effect fire. The maid enters.)

Maid
Oh Sir - such good news!! Young master Ezekiel is back from the wars out in Africa!

Mr. Grabbit
Ezekiel! Back! By the flyin' 'eck sithee tha knaws ah'm fair thraipsed and clemwarched!

Ralf
(Aside) Dammit so he wasn't killed! I paid that witch doctor for nothing! The dastard shall come into his

inheritance after all - *(thinks)* - unless I can thwart him!!

(Enter Ezekiel. He is six foot tall, strikingly handsome and ebony black. It is, in fact, not Ezekiel but a Matabele warrior who has found Ezekiel's clothes after he was eaten by missionaries. The Matabele has assumed Ezekiel's identity and has travelled back to t'North to claim his inheritance.)

Ezekiel
Jambo fada, me long time you no see.

Mr. Grabbit
By 'eck and habari Zeke. Tha's copped some sun owd lad. That's a fair tan tha's getten.

Ezekiel
Asanti sana. Fada it were hell out there, by gum sithee bwana.

Ralf
(Aside) That's never our Zeke! I could stake my life on it. Zeke had blue eyes!

Evie
Zeke my darling, you've become a proper man since you went away. You were only five foot three with fair hair and spectacles when we waved you off at Smokechester docks and now look at you.

Ezekiel
It bin all dem good foods dey gib us in Africa Mudder.

Hypnotising the Cat

Mrs. Grabbit
I'm your mother Zeke, over here, that's your younger sister.

Ezekiel
Oh yes mam - dese eyes of mine bin still not too good.

Evie
Zeke, what's that thing on your head?

Ezekiel
It bin was me pith helmet. But all dem sailors on de boat took de pith out of me helmet an med it aal floppy like an ole soak rag dem did.

(Grandma Grabbit enters. It is the first time we have seen her. She carries a large ear trumpet since she is extremely deaf.)

Grandma Grabbit
What did he say?

Mr. Grabbit
He said the sailors took the pith out of his helmet.

Grandma Grabbit
I'm not surprised they took the pith - it looks bloody stupid stuck on his head like a cow clap.

Ezekiel
Dat am one bery old joke.

Grandma Grabbit
Well I'm very old! (*To Mrs. Grabbit*) Anyway who is he? Another of Evie's fancy men?

Hypnotising the Cat

·Evie
It's our Zeke.

Grandma Grabbit
Zeke! Our Zeke! Well I never! I don't remember his hair bein' that curly. You must have been eatin' yer crusts like yer owd grannie told yer.

Ezekiel
Dat bin exackertly krekt missus.

Ralf
(*Aside*) Dash it the man's an impostor! - I must unmask him. I'll test his local knowledge. (*Aloud*) Zeke, you remember old Jabez Clegg, the whipper-in of the Eccles and Weaste Rat Hounds?

Ezekiel
(*Sensing a rat*) I don bin remember nuttink since one big witch daktar fellah him banging me head wib one big assegai bwana, sithee by 'eck.

Evie
But you remember us Zeke!! I'm your sister Evie and this is Ralf your brother.

Ezekiel
(*Aside*) My brudda him fellah! I remember Bwana Zeke him say him brudda one number one bar steward. Tinks! I mus' keep me eye on him big feller - he after seein' me off. (*Aloud*) Fadda bwana it bin one long walk from Africa, I bin ready for some feather by gum sithee, tha knows.

Hypnotising the Cat

Evie

Oh please, Zeke, it's so good to have you home, before you go to bed give us one of the old songs like you used to do. You have such a beautiful tenor voice.

Mrs. Grabbit

Oh yes darling, do.

Ezekiel

(Unpacking his guitar from his case)
Well I woke up dis morning got dem low down blues
Yes I woke up dis morning an' ah do b'leeve I got dem blues
Looked under de bed
Saw dat de dog don crapped all in my shoes - lordy lordy.

Evie

(Puzzled) Zeke! Can't you sing 'The Old Rugged Cross' or 'Nearer My God to Thee' or 'Does Your Chewing Gum Lose It's Flavour on the Bedpost Overnight'?

Ezekiel

Since I bin got de bang wid de asegai I bin done only sung de Delta Blues man.

(The maid enters)

Maid

Oh Mr. Grabbit Sir, what a Christmas this is! More good news! Young master Lemuel is back from gold prospecting in Alaska.

Hypnotising the Cat

Mr. Grabbit
Lemuel! By 'eck We thought he'd died in the frozen wastes
or been horses doovers for a polar bear's lunch.

*(Lemuel enters. It is, of course, not he but an Eskimo who has
discovered the dead Lemuel's clothes under Klondyke Kate's bed
where he died in the jousts of Venus, and has assumed his
identity. He kicks off his snow shoes and goes over to Ezekiel.
They rub noses)*

Lemuel
Hello, father.

Mr. Grabbit
This is your father Lemuel - over here. *(Aside)* The poor lad
must be snowblind - God bless his little cotton socks!

*(The Eskimo wanders over to the table climbs on it and starts
eating the candles)*

Evie
Father! Lemuel's eating all the candles!

Mr. Grabbit
Well you never know what customs and tastes young men
pick up when they're out foreign our Evie. And in any case
if our Lemuel likes to eat candles then eat candles he shall
- bloody chandeliers full if he wants to!

Maid
(Rushing in) Mr. Grabbit! Mr. Grabbit! Sir, there are three
ladies outside who say that they are the Brontë Sisters and
that they are expected.

Hypnotising the Cat

Mr. Grabbit
By 'eck I forgot we were 'avin them over fer Christmas. Fetch 'em in Matilda, but keep yer eyes on the ornaments. I've heard that some of these Yorkshire lasses 'ave sticky fingers.

(Enter the Brontës)
Mr. Grabbit
Now girls, how are you? You're lookin' wonderful I must say. Not doing panto this year?

Charlotte
No, we thought we'd give it a rest, after the summer season and what with Emily putting her back out helping our Branwell with his coal round. Anne's not been well either, have you love? (*Through all of this Anne says not one word but nods dumbly*)

Emily
(*Burps loudly*) 'Scuse me. Must be them pickled eggs I had with me special haddock and chips. This'll be your family then Mr. Grabbit.

Mr. Grabbit
Eee, I'm forgetting meself. Let me introduce you. Mother, Granny Grabbit (switch her on - she's gone off again), Evie, Ralf, Lemuel and Zeke - this is the Brontë Sisters, stars of theatre and music hall and (*chuckles*) certain Swedish videos. Last seen with Mr. Kenneth Dodd at Queens Park Hippodrome in *A Little of What You Fancy Gives You Lumps.* Singers, plate spinners, tap dancers - you name it they've done it. I give you the toast of Tintwhistle, the pleasures of Pontefract and the darlings of Droylsden. (*They raise their glasses - the Brontës nod demurely*)

Hypnotising the Cat

Charlotte

Who is the gentleman in furs?

Mrs. Grabbit

That's our Lemuel, he's back from panning for moose in Alaska.

Emily

And the dark gentleman?

Mrs. Grabbit

Our Zeke, he's just back from prospecting for lead in Africa.

Charlotte

And the hunchback with the long white beard, the cauliflower ear and the ear trumpet?

Mrs. Grabbit

That's my mother - Granny Grabbit. She's been like that since there was a cave-in at the pit she used to work at. She held the roof up for four hours while all the other colliers escaped.

Emily

So the strain of holding up a mile and a half of Lancashire coal bent her spine for ever - how brave - and look at her poor ear!

Mrs. Grabbit

The lads did that knocking her in place with a shovel. Clumsy devils! I told them to use a mallet. 'You can't knock a pit prop in with a shovel,' I said, 'You'll bend it.'

And they did. Men - they won't listen! And it was her best shovel they used too!

Mr. Grabbit
Nah cum on sithee by 'eck, tha'd fratch a ferret wi' all thy natter. It's Christmas Eve and we're staring t'work 'ouse in t' face. *(To the Brontës)* Wot about givin' us a bit of a turn you lasses. Cheer us up a bit?

Ralf
(Lasciviously staring at Emily's embonpoint) Absolutely! Spiffing wheeze pater!

Mr. Grabbit
Thee shut thy yap and put thy eyes back in.

Emily
Why not ... come on girls! If it's good enough for Mickey Rooney, it's good enough for us. Let's do the show right here!

(They throw off their dresses to reveal fish-net tights and satin basques. They tap-dance across stage. Anne unfolds a gay line of patriotic flags. Enter a Russian pursued by a bear)

(To be continued)

● ●

Wrapping Chips in a Computer

At one time I was a total Luddite when it came to computers. 'Bag of whatsit!' I used to scoff. 'Don't need one I've got a pen and a pad', and I would wave them in the air.

Now things are very different and I am a drooling slave to technology. This little bit of nonsense you're reading now, for example, was written on an Apple Macintosh lap-top portable and sent down the phone lines from Dublin where it was written to my computer at home. So I've eaten my words a lot since then. Computers are now part of my life, I plan tours, write scripts, design book jackets, work out slide programmes and even write music on one. But they're still only useful tools.

According to a new article on developments in computing we will all be able to saw off our legs and live at home with our computers doing everything for us. We'll be able to sit in our little cells and, with a special widgit on our keyboard, we'll be able to track along the high street on our screens, turn left into the mall, choose a shop we want to shop in, go through the door and browse along the shelves picking out the items we want. All while we're sat in front of the fire. When you've got what you want, you use a swipe card on a slot on the top of the telly to buy your 'stuff'. We'll be able to play video games with a friend in New Zealand, dial up home movies and music; we'll be able to book holidays, having a quick shufftie first at the resort we fancy and the actual bedroom we'll be kipping in. We'll even be able to get newspapers over our computers and have them updated by the hour, down-loading the pages we want on to the printer.

But you can't carry a computer on the bus and read it standing up, you can't sit in the khazi with a computer on your knee reading it while the foreman wonders where you are, you can't wrap chips or flatten flies with a computer, and you can't cut a computer up into squares, put a string through it and hang it on the back of the thunderbox door. You can't even amuse the kids by bending it and tearing it and turning it into a tree or a line of clowns. When I've finished my newspaper columns I squeeze them down the phone lines courtesy of e-mail and they appear as if by magic on the great steam-powered computer there in the heart of Manchesteropolis. Then the famous editor with his green eyeshade and elastic thingies on his shirtsleeves gets hold of them and, with scissors and paste, turns them into works of literature. So far most of the articles have arrived safely. But I got a frantic phone call from my editor one week telling me that there was no article in the Harding Bin on the big computer. According to my figures I was well up to date which means that a whole article of a thousand words has vanished somewhere!

I puzzled all week about that article. I mean a thousand words is a lot of words to lose, it takes a lot of dead brain cells to make a thousand words. Then I read an article on CYBERSPACE. 'What the chuff is CYBERSPACE', I hear you ask, and I have to admit that I'm not too sure myself. But it seems that with an ordinary computer and a code number, for the price of a local call you can tap in to a vast network of computers all over the world and do everything from check up on airline timetables to order a Flying (bicycle-powered) Balti Chicken delivery service. This, I thought, is for me.

So I paid a few bob for my own personal code and password, tapped in my commands and got my computer linked up to the INTERNET (that's this information superhighway-thingy whatsit that takes you into CYBERSPACE). The screen glowed with little numbers and letters, then ten mystery fingers out in the beyond of the electronic cosmos tapped in.

WHO YOU ARE?

I didn't want whoever it was to know my real name so I tapped in ERIC (sounds such a safe name - sort of vicar's and brass band conductor's name, you know what I mean) then I asked it who IT was.

HARROW ELIK - ASSUMOTO HARAKINAWA IN TOKYO IS ME. I NUMBER ONE ASHTRAY DESIGNER FOR SUZUKI CARS. WHAT LIKE WEATHER IS THERE? IT AM HERE RAINING.

IT AM HERE RAINING ALSO I tapped back in homage to Tony Hancock and his radio ham sketch.

WHERE LIVE YOU?

I had a sudden moment of panic. Would a family of Japanese Sumo wrestlers suddenly arrive on the doorstep looking for a free holiday?

THE OUTER HEBRIDES.

The screen went blank for a moment and then

HOW DO MANCHESTER UNITED? appeared. IN TOKYO NEWSPAPER SAY RYAN GIG AND CANTONA TO GET MARRIED!!

I tapped in NOT TO EACH OTHER - hoping to scotch another ugly rumour in the bud.

YOU MAKE YOLK? And yes, I had to admit I had made a yolk, however feeble. It was while we were tapping away thus to each other that another mystery hand joined in on the CYBERCHAT.

ANYBODY KNOW THE WAY OUT OF HERE?

WHO ARE YOU? I asked.

LORD LUCAN, SALMAN RUSHDIE, SHERGAR, CAPTAIN OATES AND THE CREW OF THE MARIE CELESTE. WE'RE STUCK IN HERE WITH NOTHING TO READ BUT A LOAD OF GIBBERISH WRITTEN BY SOME MANCUNIAN PRAT!!

The secret of the missing article solved! I switched off and left them all still in there, Mancunian prat eh?

Hypnotising the Cat

The next time I logged on to the Internet somebody tried to sell me a car, a 1967 Bond Minicar to be exact. I don't know if you remember the Bond Minicar. It was a sort of 250cc cheese wedge and made the Reliant Robin look like a Lexus. It had three wheels and the engine, which lived on the front wheel, was a two-stroke, single-cylinder affair only found normally on motor bikes. On the early models you had to lift up the bonnet and cock your leg inside to kick-start it. It looked as though you were trying to kick something that had crawled inside during the night to death. It had no reverse gear so parking was a bit of a bugger, and the weather sealing didn't last very long, so that in cloudbursts you had to keep bailing it out or you drowned. I had one myself and though I laugh at it now, to be fair it did turn in its own circle and was the only car to get out of our street when there was a lot of snow about one year. Still, all in all, it was a strange car. It was so low slung that you had to wind your windows up when you were stopped at traffic lights in case a dog cocked his leg up at the window.

Thinking about that little three-wheeler got me to thinking about other cars I've owned. I once had a Skoda before the Lada upstaged them as a joke. In the early nineteen seventies they were still being made part-time on the assembly line that turned out tanks for the Russian army, so they were very robust and solidly made but they had one drawback, they had a tendency only to want to go towards the west. Whether they were attacking or defecting I don't know. They were cheap, that was about all you could say for them. They were very basic. The one I had sported sash windows and a thatched roof. It looked so pretty I put garden gnomes on the running boards to set it off. The electrics were a bit primitive, you switched the indicator on and a chicken wing flopped up out of the door panel to point the way you were going, and the radio was very good - if you liked Bulgarian folk-dance music and wanted to know the number of tons of beet produced by the last five-year plan.

I had a great night out with a mate of mine the other night, Taffy Thomas the story-teller. He travels around the country giving story-telling sessions in schools and art centres and once even peddled an ice-cream tricycle round Belfast with a seat where the freezer used to be and sign on the front saying 'Stop Me And Hear One' - and people did. He has a van with a sign painted on the side with a picture of Taffy with his nose growing longer, like Pinocchio's. Taffy has been a pal for years, from the halcyon days of the British Folk Revival, and is the only man who's ever got me breathing fire and bingo calling - both stories worth telling in their own right - some other time perhaps. Taffy told me about a little boy in the first year infants' class in his home village of Grasmere. He was a farmer's boy, a 'reet Cumbrian lad', who at the end of every prayer said 'Nah then' instead of 'Amen' because that was the way he'd heard it. He'd kneel there, all of four years old, chanting away with the others ' ... for thine is the kingdom the power and the glory, for ever and ever - nah then.'

That story reminded me of my best friend Pete at St Anne's Crumpsall who learned the Hail Mary prayer and took away a wonderful surreal version to his mother. The Hail Mary goes 'Hail Mary, full of grace, the Lord is with thee, blessed art thou amongst women and blessed is the fruit of thy womb, Jesus.' Now that's quite heavy stuff for a little five-year-old to get his head around and when Pete went home that night his mum asked him what he'd learnt at school that day. 'Amongst women' and 'fruit of thy womb' had gone totally beyond the pale of Pete's psycho-linguistic world. He thought for a minute then said:

'We learned a big prayer and it was all about this lady called Mary who's covered in grease and there's a monk swimming in a room with Jesus' fruit in it.'

Zorba Chuck and the Lady from Scunthorpe

I am writing this under a sun umbrella outside a taverna on the Greek Island of Rhodes. I got a cheap deal at the last minute, £99 for seven days including accommodation. They don't tell you that the accommodation isn't finished yet and there's a cement mixer in the bedroom, but never mind, the whole deal is cheaper than a Silver Service rail ticket from Manchester to London so what the Hades!

I've been to Greece before, lots of times, mainly to the islands. One of the first places I went to was Cephalonia. I was staying in a tiny villa halfway up a mountain that overlooked a tiny harbour on what was then a quiet unspoilt island.

One night at a little harbourside taverna, where you bought your fish by weight from the tavern owner who then grilled it over charcoal and served it up with village bread and wine and a bowl of salad, I got talking to the captain of the dredger that chugged up and down the harbour all day taking out the silt and doing whatever else dredgers do. I use the expression 'talk' with some liberty because he spoke no English and my Greek was pages one to seven of the BBC *Get By In Greek* book, e.g. *'Kalispera, Eyna trapeza para quatro, parakalo'* - 'Good evening I'd like a table for four please'.

And beyond, 'How are you?' and, 'I wonder could you be of assistance, you see my friend, my wife has been eaten by a shark', that was it. So we sat there drinking wine, watching shooting stars fall into the inky sea and getting more and more friendly. Then he reached in his pocket and pulling out a mouth-organ started to play it.

Hypnotising the Cat

All the local people got up and began waltzing and tango-ing as though they were auditioning for *Come Dancing*. I signalled to my friend the dredger captain that I too had a mouth-organ and that it was up in my room at the villa. 'I go to get it,' I enunciated slowly and loudly somehow imagining (am I alone in this?) that if only we talk slow and loud enough to foreigners they will understand us. He nodded and smiled obviously thinking - if I nod and smile he will go away and stop shouting at me so loudly and slowly.

I left the little taverna with its lights shining on the water and began the long slow climb up the zig-zag dirt track to my villa hundreds of feet above the sea. Climbing it sober was bad enough, but at three in the morning with a hundredweight of fish and retsina sloshing about inside me, it was murder. I arrived at the villa a sweat-drenched, dizzy wreck, picked up the mouth-organ and set off down the hill again. The mountainside was in total darkness. Below, far below, were the lights of the little bar and, faint and sweet, I heard the strains of a waltz and the sound of happy voices singing.

I decided to take a short cut. Instead of the zig-zag track I would go straight down through the terraces of olive groves. In the blackness of night I jumped from terrace to terrace, getting closer and closer to the warmth and coMr.adeship of the little bar. A few hundred yards from the harbour I jumped from one terrace to another below. The ground suddenly exploded beneath my feet with a noise like a thousand devils. 'Eeeeeeooorrgh!! Eeeeeeooorrgh!! Eeeeeeooorrgh!!' it went, sucking in buck-etfuls of air between every scream. It took me a long time to explain to my friend the dredger captain, with the help of mime and drawings on paper serviettes, that his friend the English mouth-organ player had just jumped on a sleeping donkey.

Hypnotising the Cat

I like the Greeks, I think they are lovely people and I think that the Isles of Greece are very beautiful, in parts. Some bits, however, look like Basildon by the Sea and were probably designed by the same architect. A place I stayed at near Rhodes a few years back definitely was. If you flushed the toilet not only did nothing go away, it all came back and brought a lot of other people's stuff with it too. The hot tap ran brown sludge and the cold tap ran scalding hot water from the sun panel on the roof. I sat on the only unbroken chair on the night we arrived as the long-haired person who shares my bed was fighting with the plumbing, and suddenly before my very nose the hearthrug started moving. I had drunk several glasses of Metaxa admittedly, but I had drunk Metaxa before and, though I had got loud and silly and had become convinced that I had superhuman powers, I had never seen a moving hearthrug. I took a closer look. It was not in fact a rug but a carpet of ants that were making sharp work of a lot of sugar that had been spilt by the departing guests, a nice couple from Croydon called Arthur and Tracey. Arthur worked in a light bulb factory and Tracey was a chiropodist. They had three grown-up children and seven grandchildren and a dog called Trevor who was in kennels. They had had a lovely week but Arthur's verruca had given him a lot of trouble through sand getting in it. We learnt all this as we were waiting for Arthur and Tracey's tour bus to come and take them to the airport. It was two hours late. Had it been any later we would have got round to Arthur's golf handicap, his time as a Boys' Brigade leader and Tracey's hysterectomy. Arthur and Tracey, whatever else they told us, did not tell us about the ant carpet. I brushed the carpet on to the porch and the chickens from next door ran and ate them. 'Yum yum,' they must have thought. 'Sugared ants!' I wondered idly if they would end up with caries in their beaks. But I couldn't picture a chicken at the dentist's anyway so I gave the thought up.

Hypnotising the Cat

Metaxa, for those who of you who haven't tried it, is wonderful stuff. It's a form of Greek brandy and is made from distilled sugared ants. It has a terrible effect on me and has induced me over the years to do all kinds of strange things. One night in Cyprus, fuelled by Metaxa, I became convinced that I could swim to Turkey and set off to do so. It was only when I got a good way out and realised that what I had taken to be the lights of a Turkish town were in fact the lights of a huge Liberian tanker, that I swam back to my friends on the beach. They had drunk not wisely but too well and were not at all bothered that I might have drowned. In fact they had forgotten all about me and, as I emerged from the sea all dripping and gasping, thought I was another German coming to put an early morning towel on the sun-loungers and told me to eff off. On another occasion when Metaxa had rearranged some of the neurons, I became absolutely certain that there was nothing so simple as Greek dancing and got up on to the dance floor of the taverna we were dining at to help out two very fit Greek men who sported red boots and huge moustaches and did interesting things with a handkerchief, jumping up and down kicking their legs about. After I had completely cleared one table of its bottles and glasses and had terrorised a group of retired clippies from Glasgow with my high kicks and spirited whoops, the landlord of the Taverna came from behind his bar and, taking me for a German, told me to eff off.

I was on Cyprus one year, touring the RAF bases with a lot of other artistes entertaining the troops, when the following true story happened. One of the artistes (who I shall call Eric, to avoid a court case) bored the crust off everybody in the bar one night by telling us all how he had just bought some land in the hills above Famagusta and was going to build himself a villa there. He went on and on about this, implying that the rest of us, who didn't have land in Greece, were poltroons, hop-o-my-thumbs and ne'er-do-wells. A few months later, a bunch of us, Eric included, were working back in England at a big folk festival in the south and we were all in the hotel waiting to do our turn when the news of the Turkish invasion of Cyprus came on the television. There was not much about that sad event that could be called funny, but as we watched the Turks digging in on the mountains above Famagusta, someone said loud enough for us all to hear, 'Hey Eric, that looks like your front garden they're digging up.' Eric was not best pleased.

Three days into this present holiday, I am lying on the bed in the villa, covered, toenails to curly locks, in inch-thick, after-sun lotion, looking like a well-done trout in filo pastry and feeling as though somebody has given me a good going over with a blowlamp. My skin is so hot that a piece of newspaper placed on my thighs would burst into flames within fifteen seconds and my nose feels like it's been sand-blasted, steam-cleaned and used as a brake for runaway trams. It's my own fault of course, I should have been more careful, but the Lady from Scunthorpe got me so agitated that I left my glasses in the villa and went on the beach without them.

     With glasses my eyesight is pretty good. Without glasses? Well, a kindly optician once told me that I would be better off with another pair of ears on the front of my head. I can see things two inches from my nose and that is it. Beyond that I come up against a visual force field, faces become pink blurs, any print less than four feet high becomes a black smudge and anything further than the end of my arms vanishes into the parallel universe of Myopia. Small wonder then that I grabbed the wrong bottle off the kitchen worktop and covered myself with the olive oil I'd bought for cooking instead of the factor fifteen Ambre Solihull I'd bought in the Duty Free. I thus turned myself after several deft dollops into a giant doner kebab in a pair of swimming trunks and, after four hours in the sun, I was done on all sides and microwaved through.

Of course I didn't notice it until later when I went back to the villa to get some money for a drink. It was while searching for my wallet through the various clothes I had worn the day before that I first noticed the smell. Somebody somewhere was having a barbecue I thought - then I thought again, it seemed a little early for a barbecue. Then I realised that the scent of roast pork was coming from me and, looking in the mirror, caught sight of 'The Creature from the Bright Scarlet Luminous Lagoon.'

Then I took my trunks off and noticed that the white bits looked like a pound and a half of badly wrapped tripe surrounded by ten stone of prime beef and wondered idly whether I shouldn't have walked further along the beach to the nudist bit. An hour later, as the pain started to get to places even Heineken can't reach and my body started to look like a carelessly dropped lorry-load of pork crackling, I was ever so glad I hadn't bared my all to the great God Sol. And so here I lie, face down in the villa, shivering and burning and cursing the Lady from Scunthorpe.

The Lady from Scunthorpe? Well, she is such stuff as nightmares are constructed of. She calls every Greek man she meets 'Zorba' or 'Dimitri' or 'Chuck', and pinches the waiters' bottoms as they pass, whooping loudly with every pinch. To top it all she grabs them, after they have served her drinks, and shoves a pourboire down the waistband of their ever-so-tight matador pants. The embarrassed boys walk off with loose change rolling down their trouser legs across the pavements and down the grids. Last night she clenched a rose between her teeth and told everybody in the taverna that she had come here to get herself some Greek 'rumpo' and would die in the attempt. As an embarrassed fellow Northerner, I contemplated braining her with a plate of kalimari and chips but decided against it, since I've heard that Greek prisons make Strangeways look like The Everglades Retirement Home Bournemouth.

So what did the Lady from Scunthorpe do to make me forget my glasses? Only this. She appeared topless at the door this morning and asked me to 'unbung her lavvy'. Now I am no Adonis and would certainly not want to strut my stuff around any place where there were connoisseurs of the human form in attendance, so far be it from me to criticise anybody else's corpus, but let me tell you that the Lady from Scunthorpe has such bosoms as would have made her a stranger to her knees and feet for some time. The Lady from Scunthorpe also has Mild and Bitter tattooed on the aforementioned bosoms and to cap it all had lost her dentures down the lavatory the previous evening, while having a serious talk with Hughie and Ruth down the Great White Telephone.

Now I am not, as I said, God's gift to anything, but the sight of the Lady from Scunthorpe in full toothless flow, with a mouth like a giant sea clam on speed, muttering about lost dentures with Mild and Bitter joggling under my nose in the Greek sunshine was more than my hangover could take, so I pointed her in the direction of the 'Sun Mad' Holiday office and went off to the beach *sans* optical crutches.

So now here I lie, 'Burned, Bothered and Bewildered', head thumping and nauseous from too much sun while fourteen Greek plumbers outside employ road drills to dig up the drains of villas in search of the dentures of the Lady from Scunthorpe. And as if that is not bad enough, the Lady from Scunthorpe is there with them drinking a bottle of ouzo and calling them all Zorba Chuck and Dimitri Chuck and singing 'Una Paloma Blanca' while accompanying herself on a tin tray. If there is a God then I fear he has forgotten me.

● ●

Hypnotising the Cat

Back in Rainy City

I sn't it funny how once you've been home for a couple of days the holiday you just had starts to seem distant and unreal as though it never happened at all? The blue skies and clear seas are replaced by grey skies and diesel fumes and the people who asked you why your nose is falling off and called you a jammy devil for having a holiday in the first place, are acting as though nothing has happened and life at work and at home trundles on in the same old way. The cricket is rained off again at Headingley and Spiro and Mikhailis will still be out there on their Greek beach putting out the ranks of brollies and sun-loungers and another lorry load of marble-white and spotty English people will be lying there covered in Ambre Solihull oil like a regiment of oven-ready chips. Christostomos and Dimitri will be winking over the bar at Sharon and Tracey in their boob tubes and 'follow me home and shag me' shoes, and Emilias will be sweeping the disco floor getting ready for another night of Bang Bang Boom Boom music.

'Wednesday is fresh meat day,' said one local to me. And when I asked him why the meat wasn't fresh every day he said, 'My friend, this is not the meat you eat - this is the meat you go to bed with.' For a moment I had a mental image of Dimitri lying under a sheet with a couple of pounds of pork and a bag of lamb chops and wondered if chitterling abuse was a crime in Greek law, and then I realised that the meat he was talking about was English girls and that he and his mates see the great silver birds that fly over from England every Wednesday as flying refrigerated Nooky wagons. We live in interesting times.

Still, it was nice in a way to get back and find that nothing had really changed. People are still obsessed with the lottery and Michael Heseltine is still waffling on about arms deals with corrupt and murderous regimes as though he's explaining the rules of the under-sevens' sack race to a gang of confused parents. The lottery fascinates me. In the days of the great and corrupt Roman Emperors, when the plebeians of Rome were getting restless and there was a very real danger of revolution and change, the authorities decided to divert the attention of the proles from such matters as unemployment and insecurity by giving them bread and circuses. The bread just about kept them alive and the circuses, with the chariot races, the gladiators hacking lumps off each other and the lions moaning, 'Not Christians again - we had Christians yesterday and the day before. I hate Christians, they're all stringy and tough, why don't they give us a couple of Zoroastrians for a change?' kept their minds off all the issues. So the Romans had fat lions and Ben Hur, we've got the lottery. I have never bought, nor will I ever buy, a lottery ticket. Not because I don't believe in gambling, nor because I think you've more chance of catching John Major in bed with Margaret Beckett than you have of winning the lottery, but because I think it's a con. It raises false hopes in people, takes more money off those who can least afford it and really diverts attention from the fact that after creating an army of the unemployed, after selling off Telecom, Water, Electricity and Gas to the Fat Cats, after ruining a good railway system and a great National Health Service, after turning one of the best education systems in the world into a battleground and leaving millions of home-owners with millstones round their necks, the best that this bunch of spivs and time-share salesmen that run the country can come up with is a raffle.

And since, at the start of this diatribe I mentioned arms dealing, can I say that I'm less concerned with the dirty tricks and government guideline twisting than I am with the very principles behind the business of arms manufacture. If I sell you an axe believing that you are going to cut a tree down and you use it to butcher the mother-in-law, then my conscience is clear. If I make an anti-personnel mine that is designed to maim a civilian population or sell chemical weapons and torture implements knowing that there is every chance they will be used to prop up a corrupt dictator, then surely I am as guilty as he who uses it. It may be naive of me, and perhaps I could be accused of not living in the world of *realpolitik*, but I think people like Aitken and Heseltine should be less concerned with government procedure and more concerned with the root morality of the world arms trade. Saying, 'If we don't sell them somebody else will', is no justification. Why not follow that argument to its logical conclusion and fly out to the third world and maim and massacre the people yourself, thus cutting out the middle man and taking all the blood money yourself? But perhaps I see things too simply. I was after all a child of the sixties.

● ●

Welcome to Englandland PLC

I drove up to Newcastle the other day for a gig and on my way up driving through North Durham I saw a sign by the road: 'You are now leaving Catherine Cookson Country and entering Hadrian's Wall Country.' That sign intrigued me. It brought back a flood of memories. Last summer I went walking in the hills near Haworth in an area now known as Brontë Country; to get there I'd passed through Last of the Summer Wine Country and Pendle Witch Country. Earlier this year I went to the south-west of England and travelled through Lorna Doone Country and Thomas Hardy Country. On that drive north through Hadrian's Wall Country it struck me that the whole of Britain is being parcelled and packaged, with local tourist boards tearing their hair out trying to think of famous sons and daughters who might put a gloss on their area and attract coach loads of devotees to wobble round drinking tea and buying souvenirs.

If this thing gets any worse we're going to end up with the whole country being turned into one giant theme park - Englandland - and we'll all be employed to wobble round in whatever the image makers at the tourist board imagine to be the traditional dress of the area. We in the industrial North, in Love on the Dole Land, will wander round with flat hats, white mufflers and clogs, kicking whippets along the road shouting, 'Sithee By 'Eck tha knaws' at the passing tour buses. The last remaining rows of terraced houses in Salford will be preserved as The Taste of Honey Experience with two of them knocked together to serve jam butties and mugs of tea sweetened with condensed milk. The lost art of donkey-stoning the step will be demonstrated at two-thirty each afternoon, while out-of-work drama students will black-lead grates, poss clothes in set pots and crank mangle handles singing George Formby and Gracie Fields songs all the while. I suppose it provides somebody with a job thinking up titles like Lowry Country and Wainwright Country but what an insult to the rest of the people who lived there. Did nobody but Catherine Cookson, the Brontës, or Thomas Hardy live in those places? What about everybody else? Don't they count?

If (God forbid) I ever have a sudden brainstorm and write a series of gusset-ripping novels set in North Manchester and retire on the proceeds to die rich and Tory-voting in Thornton Cleveleys, then I hope the picturesque spa fishing village of Crumpsall on Irk where I was born is saved from the Heritage Industry's clutches. I can see it now: 'Come to Harding Country where the dramas and passions of the North burn and smoulder beneath the grimy surface!' Harding Country! What about everybody else who lived in Crumpsall? What about my mate Wharfie who could pee seventeen bricks high when he was ten and who once decided to play barbers and shaved the heads of all the girls in our street? What about old Reg who used to come home drunk from the Swan every Friday night singing 'Paper Doll' and 'Red Sails in the Sunset' to every lamp-post he passed? What about Doris and Eddie who ran the chip shop and who gave all the kids free scrapings? What about Fred the window cleaner who could make ping-pong balls come out of your ears and who could rip a handkerchief in two and magic it back together by blowing on it? What about Jeff Lee who burnt the house down making a pan of chips for all the kids in the street, or Kenny Fullen who could play football better than Georgie Best when he was nine but lost it through women and drink when he was thirteen? These are the unsung heroes of yesteryear who would never feature in a tourist board handout in a month of bank holidays.

I bet when Emily Brontë and Thomas Hardy were kids there were Freds and Dorises and Eddies to brighten their lives, but do they get a mention in the flash brochures on Hardy Country and Brontëland? - no. And the books don't tell you that Charlotte Brontë once won a peeing highest up the wall competition at Howarth Junior Mixed Infants. She got twenty-one bricks high by standing on her hands.

● ●

Hypnotising the Cat

A lnwick is a bonny town north of Newcastle, just below the border with Scotland. It has a massive city gate, the remains of fortifications built in the days when the Scots, armed only with claymores and sporrans full of porridge, would sortie across the border to raid for cattle, women and good beer. This was of course before somebody invented mealey pudden, the Broons and Jimmy Shand and the White Heather Club to keep them all in on a Saturday Night. I did a gig at the Playhouse, a nice little theatre, and noticed that following me later in the season was a French Hypnotist, Henri Du Pantalonmerde. Now, when I was a schoolboy I once sent off for a book on hypnotism advertised in the *Wizard* comic. The advert was flanked by offers of thousands of stamps for three and ninepence from a firm in Bridgnorth, Shrops and another advert for something called a 'Seebackascope', a sort of periscope that was supposed to be for Junior Sleuths but which we all knew allowed you to spy on courting couples.

The hypnotism offer had a drawing of an Eastern gentleman in a turban called Swami Somethingorother, and from his eyes and fingers powerful rays were emanating and landing on the mesmerised features of a swooning Doris Day lookalike. There was no question why steaming pubescent schoolboys like myself were sending off for this book in their trembling thousands. It was not to hypno-cure their grannies of sciatica, nor was it to banish forever Aunty Polly's arachnophobia so that she could pluck a tarantula off a bunch of Salford Dock bananas as good as the next man; it was so they could say to Bridie O'Connor, in the ping-pong room of St Fiacre's church youth club, 'You are very sleepy, you are very sleepy, undo your blouse and show me your pointy bits'.

Hypnotising the Cat

I sent off for the book hoping to cure my Gran's sciatica. It was a slim volume and most of it seemed to be a historical account of mesmerism through the ages, from The Egypt of the Pharaohs to the Great Crapoutski. I leafed through it eagerly and there at the end was what I wanted, the single lesson that would turn me into the Svengali of Crumpsall. It was all about making passes in front of the subject's eyes and dominating them with your will by using your own steely gaze. It went on at great length about these passes, and particularly emphasised that the steely gaze must be accompanied by a mysterious all-knowing smile.

I practised a few passes in the mirror, waving my hands about as though I was trying to dry them in slow motion and then I went straight to work on my smile. This was more difficult. I twisted my mouth up at one corner, lowered my eyelids until they almost covered the pupils and raised one shoulder in what I thought was a louche but commanding manner. I looked like Quasimodo after seventeen pints of Boddingtons, a King Prawn Tikka Masala and a ride on the Revolution. I set off to hypnotise my first subject, the cat. It was sitting in its usual position on the coalshed roof waiting for sparrows to land for the crumbs my Gran threw there. My Gran wasn't a cruel woman, just unlearned in the ways of moggies. Our cat pretended it was a vegetarian and kept well out of the way until the breadcrumbs were in place when it would appear to sit like Patience on a monument waiting for the Sparrowburger Flying Delivery Service to do its stuff. I stood on the dustbin, my eyes level with the cat's. I put on my power smile and fixed my eyes on her. She yawned and then looked at me as though to say, 'Do me a favour Pal and bugger off. I'm waiting for my dinner to land.'

I made a pass, then another one. I intensified my smile. The cat shifted nervously. This was something beyond her ken. I made another pass. She narrowed her eyes. She had never really trusted me since, at age six, I had put her in Mr. Dalton's motorcycle sidecar, innocently thinking that a day out would do her good. Halfway to work in Trafford Park, Mr. Dalton had dismembered his 500cc Norton, convinced that either his chain was coming off or that his pistons had dried and were about to come through the cylinder head. It was, of course, only the cat explaining that a day out in Trafford Park was not his idea of heaven. I made another pass and brought my face to within inches of the cat's. The cat's eyes narrowed still more. I intensified my smile. 'You are very sleepy,' I said.

Dettol is a very effective disinfectant handy for all cuts, grazes and scratches but it doesn't half sting. 'Don't be such a mardy,' said my Gran. 'It's only a scratch. You shouldn't have been aggravating it. It could have had your eye out. And it's a wonder you didn't crack your skull open falling off the dustbin like that. What were you doing standing on the dustbin in the first place?'

Later that afternoon, as my Gran was reading the *Universe* in her chair, I approached her staring forcefully at her and smiling and making passes. She was almost eighty at the time but came from the tenements of Dublin and could still pack a punch. Dettol on a split lip really hurts.

After a disastrous experience with Bridie O'Connor in the ping-pong room of St Fiacre's youth club, I threw the book on the back of the fire and sent off for another one on throwing your voice that showed speaking laundry baskets and people standing around in an open-mouthed group as a postbox shouted rude words at them. That one nearly got me killed.

It came to me, thinking about hypnotism, that those people who get regressed into past lives under the influence always discover they were highwaymen or courtesans or were alive during a revolution or some kind of world-shattering event like the building of the pyramids. You never get people regressing into ordinary everyday kind of lives. 'Well, I worked for fifty years for ICI Blackley making the dye that they put in tins of peas to keep them green, and then I did a bit of allotment when I retired and had a heart attack pulling a cabbage. The wife was most upset, they had to open a tin of peas.'

• • • • • • • • • • • • • • • • • • • •

The Sumo Wrestler's Diet

I had a shower in a three and a half-star hotel in the Lake District the other day. It was one of those experiences Mankind, and this one in particular, can well do without. One moment the water was fine, just the right temperature and coming out of the rose with plenty of force, just the thing to get rid of those cobwebs that are induced by the Guinness Spider. There was one of those free packets of shower gel that you have to rip open with your teeth, leaving a nasty soapy taste in your mouth, but no matter, in seconds there were suds in all the right places and I was a happy little camper. Then, I don't know what happened, somebody four miles away must have flushed the toilet or something because all of a sudden the cold shut off and the water turned into superheated steam, the kind of stuff they use for getting fifty years of gunk off truck engines. I screamed but at such a high pitch that no human ear could detect it (though I did read afterwards that flocks of bats were suddenly seen flapping round Windermere and sheepdogs above Grasmere suddenly sprinted all the way to Windscale/Sellafield and ran into the sea. They are now luminous and can work perfectly at night, though they do cause the television to change channels when they walk past). I had only been in this hotel a few hours and I had taken little notice of my surroundings, so that I found I was having great difficulty trying to turn the shower off while covering the most delicate bits of the old corpus. I stood in the corner so that only my feet and knees and the backs of my hands got poached, and butted the controls hard. Immediately, the water temperature dropped from one hundred and twenty degrees to minus six and icy needles of Lakeland mountain water caused my rib-cage to contract so much that I now had the lung capacity of a small canary, my heart decided to stop beating until it was safe to do so again, and the bits of the body I had been protecting were now so small that I could have made a batting box out of half a ping-pong ball.

In a state of shock verging on delirium I fell out of the shower and staggered across the room gibbering and shivering at the exact moment that the maid came in with my breakfast. She was a young lady in her early twenties not used to the sight of naked short-sighted men without their glasses on running towards them squealing like a banshee and looking like a nude Japanese sumo wrestler on Ecstasy. She screamed, threw the tray in the air and bolted. My already over-stimulated body now had a mél-lange of poached eggs, marmalade and porridge to deal with. It was not happy, particularly since sorting it all out meant getting back into the accursed shower stall once more. It was on getting out for the second time that I did something I have not done for a long time, ie. examined my body in some detail. It was not a happy experience. None of us are getting any younger; you, dear reader, as you peruse this little essay are piling on the nanoseconds and the seconds and the minutes, and bits of you that once pointed pertly and proudly upwards are beginning that downward slide that will leave them looking not at flies on the ceiling but at the crumbs on the floor. There is nothing you can do to stay them. Time's Winged Chariot hurries near, nor all thy tears can call the moving finger back to erase one line etc. etc. And as I stood there looking at what was left of a fine little body that used to climb trees and play rugby and do the twist at the Plaza, I decided that I needed to diet. Nothing that a bit of abstention wouldn't sort out. I'm fit enough, I get plenty of exercise. I cut the top off my own egg and play the banjo regularly, that's exercise enough for any man. No, I didn't need more exercise, I just needed to diet a bit.

So I went to Waterstone's for a diet book. The staff there are ever so helpful if you can catch them sober. Some famous ex-cricketer who had written a science fiction novel about aliens landing at Trent Bridge had just finished a signing and there was lots of free Ozplonk, so that finding a sober bookseller proved hard. In the end I settled for one that could still speak and she found me *The Big Boy's Bumper Book of Diets*. There were fruit diets, and high carbohydrate-low fat diets, high protein-low starch diets, nothing to eat but water before noon diets, raw vegetable diets, the book went on and on about brown fat and white fat and appestats and metabolism. It was all so confusing that in the end, realising that thin people suffer from one hundred per cent mortality, I took it back and swapped it for a cook book.

I didn't give up on the diet idea though and after lots of thought and consultation with dieticians I have come up with the perfect diet. I will write a book about it ere long and make myself a fortune. The Harding Beer and Chips diet quite simply is exactly what it sounds. You eat nothing but Beer and Chips (you can of course change that to Guinness and Chips if you like) with fish and mushy peas (very low in calories), you can have as much as you like but you have to accompany it with a pint of syrup of figs a day. You will lose stones in weeks.

● ●

Hypnotising the Cat

Tally Ho Yoiks Don't You Know

I t's nice to know that some things never change in this
world of ceaseless turmoil and pain, that amidst all the
hurly-burly and the chaos, some things just go on
going on, immutable and steadfast. It's all quite reassur-
ing really, in its own little way. There are some things, for
example, that are quintessentially English, that make this
island nation what it is and without which it would be
somewhere else like Iceland or Bratislava. One thinks of
the White Cliffs of Dover, the Tower of London, Mr.
Major's 'long shadows across county grounds', Bovril and
Horlicks and Fortnum and Mason's Gentleman's Relish,
and one thinks of course of Peregrine Worsthorne. I had
hardly given Peregrine Worsthorne a thought for a long
time, but last Sunday something thrust him under my nose
again. I was in North Yorkshire doing my bit for the
abolition of happiness at a little theatre, taking art and
culture to the masses of the Ridings. I did a show in a very
pleasant but small arts centre that had once been a vegetarian abattoir and then made my way to the digs. The hotel
looked like the Addams Family had just vacated it and, as
I rang the bell, the landlady opened the squealing door to
let the bats out for the night. She was dressed as for a Tory
Conference with a blue rinse, twin-set and pearls, but her
teeth looked sharper than those sported by even the most
rapacious of Lady Tories and I noticed what looked like
some Pierre Cardin bolts in her neck. But I was tired and
weary so I hoped that they were merely low-slung ear-
rings and lumbered into the hall.

I ordered an eight o'clock call and the *Observer* and
the *Independent on Sunday*, then, climbing the winding
stairs to my room I scattered garlic all round the threshold,
wound a set of rosary beads around my neck, pushed the

wardrobe against the door and collapsed on a gilt and white iron bed with curtains, swags and tie-backs under a white candlewick bedspread with large pink roses and pastel green leaves on it. If there's anything I hate more than white and gilt iron beds with curtains, swags and tie-backs, it's damn candlewick bedspreads. When I was on the road in the seventies I spent years shivering under candlewick with only that, a thin nylon sheet and an ex-army blanket between me and the Arctic winds. And those nylon sheets! All the misery of artificial fibres with none of the warmth. If you turned over too quickly blue static flashes illuminated the gloom of the bedroom, and having sex between nylon sheets could generate enough electricity to run the street lights of a small town, particularly if you were wearing wincyette pyjamas. If you got out of bed without earthing yourself your hair stood up like Ken Dodd's and all the fluff in the room floated over to you and covered you in fine fur so that you looked like a yeti, and as you put your hand out towards the cold tap a fork of lightning would stab across, discharging several thousand volts of static electricity down the piping to earth, leaving you stood naked with the charred remnants of your pyjamas round your ankles and the melted remains of a rubber waistband round your middle. Happy days. Where was I? Ah yes, Peregrine Worsthorne.

So I passed a terrible night in Blue Rinse Towers slipping in and out of a fitful sleep as the full moon coursed across the sky and the rattling of chains and the howling of ghouls in the attics made a quaint counterpoint to the screams of some wretch being dismembered in the cellar below.

At breakfast the next morning I noticed the *Sunday Telegraph* on my plate. The landlady's revenge!!
'There was no *Independent* or *Observer*,' she sneered, 'so I thought this was the next best.'

Next best? I'd rather read sandpaper!

Hypnotising the Cat

I have not taken much notice of blood sports since I gave up riding with the Salford and Weaste Rat Hounds when an old war wound began to play up, but I noticed in the *Telegraph* that the great English Catholic sportsman and intellectual Peregrine Worsthorne has recently been riding with the Heythrop Hunt. You can imagine with what interest I read of Perry's goings on. As long as there is a Perry there will always be an England of elms and rooks and old school ties and stirrup cups and Tally Whatsits ringing out across frosty fields as expensively kept dogs chase off to rip apart a lovely animal. But in his piece in the *Telegraph* Worsthorne surpassed himself. There was a West Indian steel band playing for the hunt invited by a local 'much loved horse breeder ... 'writes Perry, going on at full gallop to tell us how well the band were received and how the steel drums blended beautifully with the horns, the jingling of bridles and the baying of the hounds. Then he tells us how a sour note was struck by an old grandee saying, 'Never did I expect to hear a nigger band in these parts.'

Now, I don't believe for one moment that Mr. Worsthorne is a racist; he obviously found the old pratt's words quite shocking, but Perry being Perry he also thinks the story is a damn funny one, the kind of thing one can tell at the club after the port has gone round. Oh yes, it's nice to see that England is still England and country squires are still country squires and that God is a White Man who, when not riding to hounds, is still in his heaven. When I'm with my black friends in future I will remember the words of that fox-hunting man and think how it is a terrible pity that the French Revolution didn't quite make it over the pond.

● ●

St Patrick Goes to Vegas

S itting in the dressing-room of what was probably my worst gig for years the other night, it came to me that St Patrick's Day is upon us once again. Memories of the Paddy's Days of yore swam back across the goldfish bowl of memory, the years fell away and I was six years old again and going through the church door to mass on that saint's day with the herbage of a small upland meadow pinned to my left breast. 'That's a good bunch of sham-rock,' said Monsignor Aspinall as I went to sit with my fellow classmates, all similarly garbed. Good!! You could have fed a herd of goats off it for a fortnight. There was that much shamrock in church that day that the children of St Anne's Crumpsall looked like a gang of Japanese snipers in jungle camouflage. During the mass we sang:

Hail Glorious St Patrick
Dear Saint of our Isle
On us your poor children
Bestow a sweet smile.

It didn't seem at all strange to me that, this being the Isle not of Ireland but England, we should have been singing about St George, because, like many children of Irish extraction, the fabled land of Ireland where everything was green and pleasant and where people were conceived and lived their lives without sin, seemed much more real somehow than the streets of Manchester. I know now that the ideas we had were mostly romance and that Ireland has the same number of problems that you'll find any-where else, but in those days it seemed a land of fair men and women, music, dancing and (based upon my experi-ence with various grandads and uncles) Guinness and good conversation. Much of this is of course true and at the risk of offending the man in Salford who keeps writing letters telling me to bugger off to Ireland if I like it all that much, let me just say that it still has fine people, music, Guinness and the *craic* . Having said that, let me also say that it has exported to the world one of the worst pieces of Tomfoolery and Paddy Whackery ever in that strange phenomenon called Paddy's Day. In Ireland Paddy's Day lasts for about three hours, it's all over by lunchtime. In most of the small towns across the country there is a procession with a pipe band, a show band on the back of a trailer being towed by a lorry with something like 'Eddie Conron for your Cattle Nuts' painted on it, some school-children, some nuns, a few scouts and guides, a tubby priest or two and a goat for good luck. They process round the streets, there are a few speeches and then everybody goes home. At night time there will be a bit more music in the pubs and a bit more drinking and that will be about it. If Paddy's Day was the Bacchanalia people would have it to be, most of the children in Ireland would be born nine months after Paddy's Day which of course they are not. Nine months after the World Cup yes, but Paddy's Day - no.

Paddy's Day in Dublin this year was a hoot. After the procession everybody went home as usual, leaving thou-sands of confused Japanese and American tourists in Burberry raincoats and Aran sweaters, wandering around the streets wondering where the good time had gone. By night the town was buzzing again of course but during the day - nothing. Scraps of paper being blown along the empty streets and puzzled tourists staring into the win-dows of closed shillelagh and Aran sweater shops. In America of course St Patrick's Day is the day when every-body suddenly discovers that they are Irish. I once spent Paddy's Day in Las Vegas. It was an experience even a total amnesiac would fail to disremember. There in the heart of the Nevada desert, people were cruising the Strip dressed from tip to armpit in green and wishing everybody a 'Great Paddy's Day' in a temperature of a hundred and seven Fahrenheit with tumbleweed rolling down the street. People who had no more idea where Ireland was than what coinage the people of Ulan Bator use to buy their yak butter were singing 'Cockles and Mussels' at full lung thrust as the lights of the Silver City Saloon and Caesar's Palace flashed across the desert evening air.

My last memories that night are of being served pints of draught, fizzy, cold and foul-tasting beer that had been dyed a bright almost luminous green by a very large and very beautiful black lady who was dressed as a Leprechaun, complete with white beard, green tights, curled-up shoes with brass buckles and bells on, a pointy hat and a shillelagh. 'Are you having a great Pat's Day?' she asked as she placed the fizzling green rubbish before me. I looked around. On a table close by were four Mexicans in Aran sweaters and Donegal tweed trousers and a Cherokee Indian dressed as Mother Macree. A Hispanic pianist dressed as Napper Tandy was playing the 'Wearing of the Green' very badly on one of those horrible electric organs that have a built-in drum machine inside. You know the kind of thing. It sounds like somebody with a wooden leg kicking a wet cardboard box while he's pumping up a tractor tyre with a bike pump, all 'dunk/shish-dunk/shish-dunk/shish'. They should be banned. As he was playing, a seven-foot Texan dressed as Brian Boru who had drunk 'not wisely but too well' waddled to the microphone and began singing 'Galway Bay', only to break down in tears overcome with grief at the thought of the terrible lot of the Emigrant. I got very drunk that night because, as T.S. Eliot once said, 'Mankind cannot bear too much reality', and I was one hombre who had certainly overdosed on reality that Paddy's Day.

Dante and the Dressing-Room

S ome day I will write my autobiography and in it there will be a section about life on the road as a strolling player and in that section there will be a long bit on theatre dressing-rooms. Anybody who has strutted and fretted their hour on the provincial stages of this many-sceptered whatsit isle thingy, will know that theatre dressing-rooms can be a danger to your mental, physical and spiritual health. Nothing can destroy your sense of wellbeing more than entering a theatre on a sunny spring evening ready to do your bit for Great Art only to find that you are in a dressing-room such as must have been reserved for the Christians before first house in the Coliseum. 'No point in doing much to it Mr. Delfont - they'll all be dead in twenty minutes.'

From the stalls where Los Punteros (as we affectionately call you) sit, the stage, the little 'O' on which we weave our spells, seems a place where magic is made to happen. Backstage? Well, if magic is a sand bucket, an emphysemic stage manager smoking his way towards Nirvana and four lady dancers of a certain age, (Widow Twanky's Little Helpers) who are finishing off waxing their bikini lines at the side of the stage while waiting for their cue to enter Chinatown Barnsley, then magic has changed since David Niven shot the rabbit. I don't want to disillusion you but backstage is the engine room, the boilerhouse, the mixing shed, the unlovely limbo where the thesps, hoofers, musoes, comics, knife throwers, vents and spesh acts gird their loins before crawling on to a spatter of indifference.

Backstage is all dark and gloomy, a catacomb festooned with wires and cables and ropes, where misogynistic electricians moan about sound technicians

118

and sound technicians grope assistant stage managers behind Cinderella's coach. Beyond the thin membrane of the curtain we go to be born anew several times a night before the agog audience in our motley and slap, but once back behind the velvet, it's out with the cards and the knitting and 'What's the name of that pile ointment you mentioned last night? One of the dwarves is suffering terrible. He told Snow White last night that he was in that much pain he couldn't do the twist properly in that bit when the wicked stepmother gets her tongue caught in the mangle. He said he could only shuffle from side to side. He kept well upstage though. He didn't want her to think he wasn't giving it his all, but he said his little tush felt like he'd ridden a Harley Davidson with no saddle over forty miles of bad road.'

If backstage is Limbo then dressing-rooms can be the pits of Hell. I remember working a town hall once in a small Scots town which shall be without name. It was a foul December night and sleet and hail were being driven down from the Highland Glens by Arctic gales. As we drove into town I noticed that there were very few people about and those that were about looked as though they were the result of some dreadful genetic experiment which had gone wrong. The theatre? Well let me say that the lighting system was so old and chaotic that winding the spots up to full beam dimmed all the traffic lights in the town and plunged Nardoni's Milk Bar (the sole night life of the town) into total darkness. The seats hadn't been cleaned since the concert to welcome the soldiers returning from the war with the Boers, and the foyer still sold Fry's Five Boys Chocolate. (This was the Eighties!) The star dressing-room had a pane of glass missing from one of the windows; the antiquated heating system, which had been designed to run on English Redcoats, had packed in for the winter and a one-bar electric fire was the sole source of heat. What I thought was dandruff on my jacket shoulders turned out to be ice crystals and, when I looked in it, the fly-specked mirror with its ring of lights (only three of which worked) reflected an image of the kind of frozen wretch Wenceslas trooped after. Fag-end burns were the only decoration to break the monotony of the Formica dressing-table, and the only chair in the room was a metal tubular affair with a ruptured canvas seat and greasy back.

There was a coffin-shaped wardrobe with a single wire hanger in it and the sink, stained and cracked like an old urinal, had a blocked waste pipe from which came odours I have only smelt since emanating from the sewers of some of the worst streets in Kathmandu. When I turned on the tap it coughed and spat out a few rusty flakes before feebly disgorging some browny-yellow stuff into the bowl. The agent who had organised the concert did have the decency to send over a bottle of single malt, but I didn't know whether to drink it or use it to start a fire after I'd chopped up the wardrobe. When I complained to the manager, a man with a face like a marabou stork and the mien of a Jack Russell with a thistle up its bum, he sniffed up the dewdrop that was about to fall from his pale blue frozen nose and looked down at me. 'Elvis was here last week and he didnae complain.'

'Elvis?' I answered. 'Elvis Costello?' I reasoned that unless it was a spiritualists' convention it couldn't be Elvis Presley since he'd been dead a good few years.

'No. Elvis McCracken and his White Heather Funsters; they do a mixture of Harry Lauder, Jimmy Shand and Country and Western with a bit of humour thrown in. He wears a sequined kilt and looks exactly like Elvis. He's awfy good.'

I don't need to tell you that I didn't start a fire with that bottle of malt.

• •

Hypnotising the Cat

Charles Dickens Gave Queen Elizabeth One Here!

Travelling round doing what are known in showbiz as 'gigs', you get to develop very strange habits. Staying up late and drinking too much are a couple of them. The reason people stay up late usually is that they're so full of adrenalin after strutting and fretting their hour that if they went to bed they'd be twitching and gibbering until the grey light of dawn. The reason they drink too much is obvious - it helps you to unwind. I've seen people get so unwound at times that they've come off the spool completely. Some of them also, it must be said, 'do drugs'. Now I do not 'do drugs'. Not because I think cannabis or marijuana evil or the first step towards the needle and the white slave trade, but because anything stronger than Bisodol sends me off the planet. I was at a party once where they were handing round a joint the size of a roll of wallpaper. I took what they call a 'toke or two' and spent the next five years with my head down the toilet convinced I was going to die. It wasn't five years of course, it was eight minutes but your time scale goes all to cock with that stuff.

Your eating habits change too when you're in the biz. Most 'artistes', as we like to be known, rarely eat before a show because it slows you up. The blood that should be revitalising the crucial brain cells that make you sharp and witty, ends up swirling round the stomach helping it to deal with that big plate of tripe fricassee you've just downloaded. So most artistes tend to eat late, and the only places open after everyone has gone home and the usher-ettes are checking under the seats for lost umbrellas, handbags and false teeth, are the Indian restaurants.

Over the years I've been guided by locals to a fair

number of the good curry houses in this little island. The Kash in Bradford is still one of my favourite haunts, it has expanded over the years from a little café serving local Pakistani families, students, folkies and jazz musicians, to a huge restaurant with two floors. But it's still inexpensive and the food is as good as ever. Staying open late can have its drawbacks too, since the golden light emanating from the Chittagong Tandoori Palace can act like a beacon for those flotillas of the Great Undead who are wandering the seas of the shut-down town, full to the gunwales with Fosters Kangaroo Pee. Said's Curry Corner in Bradford will always remain in my memory as the place where I saw such a knight of the barley trying to eat his curry-soaked handkerchief while mopping his head with a chapati. The Taj Mahal in Southampton I remember as the place where a sailor who reckoned he could eat the hottest curry thrown at him went into total meltdown before our eyes, screaming for toilet rolls to be put in the freezer and almost sank through the mantle of the earth going Chinawards. And of course there is our own Curry Mile in Manchester along Rusholme Road, where you would be hard put to find a bad meal and where you can dine on the food of princes wrapped in silver foil for a lot of dosh or sample the fare of the common man for a few bobskies.

But I've noticed a new cuisine emerging over the last few years - Balti cooking. The Curry Club guide tells me that this is the cuisine of Baltistan. Let me tell you good people that I have been to Baltistan several times and nothing in the various 'Balti' cookbooks or in any of the 'Balti' restaurants I have eaten in bears the slightest resemblance to the food of that country. The last meal I ate in Baltistan was curried goat with Balti bread and the goat was so tough I seriously considered ripping off the worn soles of my trekking boots and replacing them with the meat. I lived on that kind of stuff for two months. It's good plain food, traditional Balti food. But I can't quite see that going down well with the punters in some of the new Balti houses, nothing on the menu but Old Vegetables That Have Been Carried Up The Glacier to K2 and Back Vindaloo, or Knackered Old Goat Rogan Josh With a Thick Bread Pancake. Still, you never know.

Talking of gigs (which is how all this began) I am at present in King's Lynn for the poetry festival doing my bit for the Muse and staying in a fine old coaching inn where Charles Dickens once spent the night. If all this 'So and So Stayed Here' stuff is true then Charles Dickens, Mary Queen of Scots and Bill Shakespeare must never have spent a night at home in their own beds. King's Lynn is a very bonny town, lots of old buildings and a great feeling of space. King John died here from a surfeit of lampreys but whether they were Balti Lampreys with Garlic Nan or just Lamprey and Chips with Mushy Peas nobody seems to know.

One thing I can't understand is why my mobile phone doesn't work here. Normally in mountain regions you get cut off or the reception is poor. Here in Norfolk, where the people least likely to be busy are the mountain rescue team, reception should be great. It is garbage. Last night I spoke to home only by standing in the bathroom with one foot on the bog and the other in the shower. 'What's a poet doing with a mobile phone?' I hear you say. Well, I bet you a fiver if they'd been about then, Wordsworth would have had one so he could ring up De Quincey and say, 'Have you scored any good dope Quincey? Coleridge is coming over and you know he can't write unless he's on.'

● ● ● ● ● ● ● ● ● ● ● ● ● ● ● ● ● ●

The End of the World is Nigel

S itting in the hotel dining room this morning I opened the paper to read that, according to an advertisement put in by a nun called Sister Marie, the world is going to end. I wondered whether I should order a bottle of champagne and invite the rest of the diners around me to a last-minute party and orgy. Then I looked at the three businessmen chomping on greasy eggs and strips of dead pig, the elderly couple with the hearing aids, the blonde waitress with the roots and the little Italian restaurant manager with the suit shoulders full of dandruff, and decided I was better off making a perfect act of contrition and phoning home to say goodbye. Then I discovered that the world wasn't going to end just then but soon, before the end of the millennium - probably, perhaps, definitely, maybe - it's all a little like waiting for a British Rail Inter City. Apparently, when the mighty fist of God does come it will be in the shape of a massive comet and it will destroy the world because God has sent it as his judgement on us all, in particular America - 'for poisoning the world with evil films and obscene videos'. Now, as somebody who thinks that America has done for television what Herod did for Mothercare, I must admit that I have often wished a plague of frogs or boils or death of the firstborn upon the mindless idiots that spawn *Baywatch* and *Scooby Doo*, but I don't see why the rest of us have to fry with them. Can't we just have a selective end of the world? Can't God just take out the nasties like Saddam Hussein, Rupert Murdoch, Margaret Thatcher and her indecently rich wally of a son, Mark?

Then I noticed that Sister Marie (who is only a lay helper at a London convent) is really a lady called Sofia Paprocki and that she comes from Cheetham Hill, Manchester where she had her first vision in 1956, and I suddenly realised that we are probably all safe, for a couple of millennia at least Sister Marie, who has virtually sold all her worldly possessions in order to place the advertisements in the papers, has also written songs which she has sent to Andrew Lloyd Webber (and if anybody is in need of a good song it's him) but he turned them down. Apparently he thought that lyrics such as 'I'm a nun I don't get much fun And soon there'll be none 'cos it's Armageddon,' were not quite his mug of Tetleys. I don't know, though, I can quite see Mr. Webber making a very successful musical out of the rantings of a part-time Carmelite from Cheetham Hill who prophesies the end of the world. If you can make a musical out of a right-wing Argentinian fascist dictator's mistress's obsession with uniforms, processions, suitcases and halls, I would have thought you can write a musical about just about anything. But I'm probably wrong.

I was reading an article on the modern novel the other day and discovered that a bloke called Timothy Mo was given a six-figure advance for one of his novels. It came to me that there must be some kind of gold in them there tripewriters, so I sat me down and pondered long and hard over the kind of novel I could write. It would be wonderful to write something like *Jurassic Park* or *Mrs Doubtfire* - the kind of books that are almost guaranteed to be snapped up by Hollywood and turned into a film with Robin Williams and ten million pounds worth of artificial bosoms and Tyrannosaurus Rex. I did once think that my seminal novel *Killer Budgies* would have made a good disaster movie but I sent the script addressed to Mr. Steven Spielberg, Somewhere in Hollinwood, and it was two years before the post office sent it back saying that there was no Spielberg in Hollinwood, though there were three in Prestwich and two in Sale ... but they were all dentists and didn't want to produce my film as a book, thank you. I wasn't discouraged, though, and sent *You Can See The*

Angel's Bum, Miss Worswick to Ken Loach thinking he might see it as a gritty piece of social realism and a good sequel to *Raining Stones*. But a sudden blank spot hit me while I was addressing the envelope and I sent it instead to Mr. Kev Leech, my old pal from schooldays who saw it as a slur on his character and put it in the hands of his lawyers. The trial starts next month.

I've come to realise that if I'm ever going to get anywhere as a great writer I'm going to have to write a book that has everything and I scouted round Waterstone's, treading carefully over the tired and emotional assistants. There were sex novels, sex and shopping novels, gusset-rippers, Mills and Boon, Aga sagas, Jilly Cooper bonkbusters and novels about medieval monks getting lost in libraries while trying to deconstruct the meaning of meaning. My new novel has it all - I'll leave you with the opening paragraph.

It was while Sally Goodchester was unloading groceries from the Range Rover that she noticed the tall dark handsome monk standing looking at her with his deep dark eyes. Her hand went to her throat and felt the Fabergé pendant that was nestling against her Liberty scarf. She smiled at him. 'Do I know you?'

'I've come to mend your Aga.'

Soon they were sat in armchairs either side of the newly mended stove.

'What's a monk doing mending Agas?' she asked, sipping her dry martini and eyeing his well-filled habit.

Suddenly they were in each other's arms. He carried her upstairs into the bedroom and tearing her Janet Reger underwear off - he put his own Pierre Cardin boxer shorts back on ...
(to be cont.)

•••••••••••••••••••••

Hypnotising the Cat

What Colour is Yours?

A few months back I spent three weeks working in mid-Wales making a series of programmes for Radio 4. I'd driven through the area before, making my way quickly from gig to gig, but I'd never spent much time there. It was a revelation. The place is entirely beautiful and the people were as friendly as you'll meet anywhere. They have the problems that rural communities are facing everywhere - low subsidies, falling populations, changing ways - but that aside, the roads are quiet, the towns tidy and human and the hills roll all around you in great beauty. I have many memories of that working trip that will stay with me. One is of an old man reading a poem in Welsh, standing on the very hillside he composed it on. He'd been working on the hill and it came to him, as he crossed its great shoulders, that this was the very place where Owain Glendower, the last prince of Wales, had fought one of his bloodiest and fiercest battles against the English. Old Iori stood on that windy hill and, though I have no knowledge of Welsh at all, he read so beautifully and passionately that my eyes were wet with tears.

Another time, in a bar in Machynlleth, a fierce little man, seventy years old and as broad as he was tall, told me how he'd met the friend he was drinking with in prison. I asked him what he was in prison for.

'Oh boys it was years ago now. I was a young devil in those days, up to all kind of tricks. Nothing bad mind, just mischief really. I got very drunk one day and coming out of the pub I saw a pullover on a washing line. "That would fit me fine," I said to myself and I pinched it. A bit on I saw a meat pie on a window sill. It was freshly cooked you see and the woman had put it out to cool. Boys it smelt so good it was more temptation than any man can stand.

I pinched that too. Course the bobbies caught me and they took me down to Cardiff to be tried. I only spoke Welsh then, I'd hardly any English at all. I was a bit of a rebel too, so I told them I wanted my case to be heard in Welsh. They had to delay the trial while they got an interpreter in, of course, and that didn't please the judge. Well, they got me in the dock and the judge said, "Name?" and I told them. You see in those days I used to box a bit and my fighting name was "The Flower of Wales" - so I told them that, see.

' "What did he say?" asked the judge.

' " He says he's called "The Flower of Wales,"' says the interpreter.

' "Well,'"says the judge, "tell him I've a got special little pot to put him in. Six months. " '

A couple of years back I was driving across the south-west of America in a camper van taking photographs and generally going wherever the wind took me. I'd crossed Death Valley with the fridge full of Mexican beer and I'd trekked into the Grand Canyon along the beautifully named Bright Angel Trail. Wonderful stuff. One afternoon I was cruising along the interstate through a huge Navajo reservation. A hand-painted sign caught my eye. 'Dinosaur footprints', it said. I pulled over and climbed out. There was a tin shack, desert all round and not much else. A young Indian lad came out of the shack shading his eyes against the afternoon sun. 'My name's Maurice Chee,' he said, what's yours?' I told him and we shook hands and he led me across the desert to the footprints. There preserved in stone was a set of huge claw prints, records of some giant lizard's journey across the mud flats of a primeval lake. We stayed there quite a while, it was a quiet place, Maurice was in no hurry and neither was I. I was taking some shots of the print when Maurice asked, 'Where you from?'

'England.'

'What colour are people over there?'

'All kinds of colours, some of them are white, some of them are black, some of them are coffee-coloured. There are all kinds of people.'

He thought for a moment.

'We get all kinds of people here too. I'm a red man. We get white people, black people, yellow people - all kinds. I tell you something. It don't matter what kind colour you are, red, yellow, black or white as long as you ain't an asshole. Assholes are all the same colour.'

Such sweet wisdom - Shakespeare might have written that himself.

Dyslexic Doomster

Here Comes Godot - And About Bloody Time Too!

I've always wanted to be a campaigning journalist. Not because the pen is mightier than the sword. It is not. (Try warding somebody off with a Waterman's Lac 14 carat italic oblique, when he's carrying a whacking big cutlass. The worst you can give him is mild blood poisoning and that takes a long time to get hold.) But the pen, though not mightier than the sword, can be a powerful weapon in other ways. It can get up people's noses, which at times can be all to the good, and it can raise people's awareness of matters that are troubling some of us on this mortal coil. So let me use this column to tell you about a new protest movement I have started, the SAM society. SAM stands for the Society for the Abolition of Matinees. There are only two members so far, myself and Bernard Wrigley, but we exhort all thespians reading this to join immediately. We formed the society after giving two matinee performances of *Waiting for Godot* at the Bolton Octagon. It was a wonderful play to be involved with, every evening was a pleasure, the mystery of gathering darkness, night falling over the city, the general feeling every night that things of magic were about to unfold.

The matinees were different. Performing in a matinee is like making love with your pyjamas on while stood in a bowl of cold porridge - greatly less than wonderful. We performed the play in the round with the front row of the audience sat at stage level. Shopping bags fell over and tins of Puppy Munch rolled across the stage during the most harrowing speeches. An old lady who was knitting during a terrible row between Vladimir and Estragon muttered, 'Dropped a bloody stitch' in one of Beckett's most well-written silences. The rest of the audience thought

130

she was part of the play and gave her a round of applause when she finished a particularly well-turned sleeve. We soldiered on, giving of our best, knowing that in a few hours' time we'd have to crank it all up again and strut and fret our hour for the night show.

This is cruelty to actors. Matinees must go! They were invented anyway at a time when nurses and other shift workers couldn't get to the theatre in the evening. There is no excuse for them now except for the greed of theatre managements. They are bad for the actors and worse for the audiences. Even the ancient Greeks waited until evening when the sea breezes blew the words up into the stalls. Scrooge-like theatre managers will say things such as, 'What about the kiddies, the little teenies who come to see Noddy and Postman Pat and bankrupt their parents buying tee shirts, cassettes and programmes?'

'Tish push, I bite my thumb at you,' I answer. 'Let them come at night like the rest of us and if they fall asleep we can employ jobless people to pinch them awake again.'

An added advantage of the abolition of matinees would be that actors would then be free during the day to do other things like window-cleaning rounds and school-crossing work, thus supplementing their meagre wages. I rest my case.

The show was billed as the first production outside New York to cast two comedians in the leading roles. A lot of people came therefore looking for laughs. There were a good few but, this being Beckett, they were far outweighed by the silences and by lines like, 'They give birth astride the grave. The light flickers an instant and then it is dark once more. ' In the bar after the show one night a local comedy lover raised his glass to his lips and without looking at me muttered dryly out of the corner of his mouth, 'Not many bleedin'chuckles in that was there, cock?'

● ●

Herod Where Are You Now We Need You?

I've decided that parenthood is a con, a swizz, a trick, a double-cross, a sting worked royally on us gullible humans by Mother Nature, since, without the production of offspring, the huming race would vanish off the face of the planet (and for some unfathomable reason She seems to want to keep us here.)

Did we but know what terrible monsters those pretty pink and babbling things in the hospital crib turn into, children would be avoided like the plague and all of us would be using every form of contraception known to man and womankind including 'No!!' People who are trying very hard for a family will find this puzzling, I suppose, but I stand by my words. Kids are a pain from day one. As babies they puke on you, poo on you, keep you awake at night screaming, either because they haven't had enough to eat or they've had too much to eat. And then if they go quiet you imagine they're dead and get up every four minutes to check that they're still breathing.

And babies are so expensive! In Africa where I was last year Mum just ties the baby on her back and toddles down town to market to meet the other mums and have a chat over the ochra, mangoes and breadfruit. Here a mum or dad can't move without buggy/ car-seat/ bottles/ nappies/ baby wipes/ tins of food/ baby buds/ spare clothes/ spare teats/ dummy/ rattle/ toys/ sun-hat/ baby oil/ botty ointment and who knows what else. Half the time she loads the car up and sets off, forgetting that the baby is still back in the house in its cot where she left it after changing it.

The toddler years are wonderful. They are spent:

Hypnotising the Cat

1 - with your arm down the lavatory pan looking for keys/ bankcards/ cheque books and grandad's heart tablets that they've 'posted' down it.

2 - trying to get jam butties out of the video with a breadknife and

3 - trying to get lego bricks/ dog bones/ hair clips/ scissors/ knobs off the cupboard/ the head off a Barbie doll/ the cat and whatever else the child has swallowed out of its mouth. This is known to psychiatrists as the oral stage. Girl babies grow out of it, boy babies do not.

If you survive the early years without jumping under a bus then they present you with a whole new set of endearing qualities such as:

1 - not doing homework, then sprawling on the settee in front of the TV watching some Australian dross that wouldn't tax the brain of a garden snail, looking as though somebody has removed all the bones from their body, telling you that they haven't got any homework and anyway they'll do it on Sunday,

2 - bringing their friends home so that they can sit in the kitchen all night drinking coffee and talking about whatever it is fourteen year olds find to talk about for six hours.

3 - using the phone as though it's a free service and phone bills are just a joke. She's just walked all the way home from school with her best friend and two minutes later they're on the phone to each other for three hours.

'What do you find to talk about?' you scream, the blood pressure higher than the pressure cooker just before it blew last Xmas and covered the kitchen ceiling with pudding.

'Homework,' is the sullen reply. If she was Pinocchio her nose would be a danger to low-flying aircraft.

Then there's the door-slamming stage. The most veiled and gentle hint that the lounge floor might be easier to cross without the stale sandwiches, empty mugs and tidal wave of magazines, make-up, roller skates, shoes, records and cassettes that has turned the room into an SAS obstacle course, so that you can only get from kitchen to hall without breaking a leg by climbing along the back of the settee and abseiling off the mantelpiece, ends up with a rapid exit via a door that has suddenly developed a return spring with a PSI of fifteen tons. In six months two lady teenagers of my acquaintance managed to loosen every door jamb in the house, produced settlement cracks in every house in the street and created shock waves that hit Richter Scale Six at Leeds University forty-five miles away.

Toothpaste tubes are another interesting teenage socio-pathological phenomenon. Why is it impossible for mutant nangy teenage whatzits to start squeezing a tube of toothpaste from the bottom and finish weeks later with the tube all neatly rolled up to the top like normal civilised Janets and Johns? Why do they always grip a brand new tube as though it's some kind of slug they're trying to kill and then strangle the life out of it so that the middle is all bent and squashed and the top is missing?

And don't talk to me about clothes and wet towels and hairdryers left strewn all over the floor. You come home some nights and if it wasn't for the fact that every electrical item in the house is on full whack and you can hear the strains of four of her friends singing along to *Take That* coming from the bedroom, you'd swear you'd been burgled.

And then they get to the stage where you bore them and embarrass them.

'I'll only go to the wedding/Christening party/ Barmitzvah with you if you promise not to jive or do the Twist, dad.'

'Dad do you have to make those noises while you're

eating?

'It's my house!'

'Yes and I have to live here! And when you eat like that it sounds like somebody walking through a swamp wearing wellies full of custard!'

Yes, 'tis all a con. And don't give me that 'Where would you be without them?' nonsense, because I know where I'd be. On a beach somewhere drinking ice cold pina coladas instead of bashing away at a word processor thinking, 'Two thousand words - that's the orthodontist paid, three thousand words, that's the piano lessons, four thousand words, that's the school trip.' Yet as somebody pointed out, if it were not for Mother Nature's con I wouldn't have been born either and then where would I be? Life's puzzling sometimes.

• •

You Say Tomatoes and I Say Potatoes

I'm tapping this into the little Apple somewhere over Des Moines, Nebraska on my way to New Mexico from Chicago. I'm over here taking photographs and recording music for a future TV series. But the craziest thing is that the hardest part about getting here was the journey to Manchester airport this morning. I'll go early, I thought, and avoid the traffic. So I ordered the taxi for eight o clock. Thirty-five minutes later we're still stuck in the coagulating traffic on the M56 westbound. Excuse me for being stupid but why can't the road engineers concentrate on one lump of motorway at a time and throw all their men and machinery at it until it's finished? Why do they cover miles and miles of the motorway with cones, close it down to one lane and then set one man and a boy and a pickaxe at work for three years on the whole shooting match. No doubt the men at the ministry will have an explanation for it all.

Anyway enough of that moaning. I'm always amazed, coming back to the States, how different the place is from Britain. For all the Coca-colanisation, the Big Macs, the TV programmes and the baseball caps we have in the UK now, America is still a world apart. Where else other than the USA would you find a town like Avon, Colorado where they have a Bob Fest every year? It all began when somebody asked for ideas for the name of the new town bridge a couple of years back. There were all kinds of suggestions like John F. Kennedy Bridge and Bald Eagle Bridge but the winner was Bob. So the bridge is called Bob and each year on the anniversary of its naming there is a Bob Fest and Bobs from all over America come to meet other Bobs and there are Bob-e-Ques when they roast Hot Bobs and Bob for Apples and other such fun things and then they all line up, thousands of them in front of the Bob Bridge, to have their photograph taken. Then they go away again until next year.

There is a cheeriness about most Americans that I really like. A lot of English people feel that Americans are somehow shallow or false because they tell you to have a nice day or invite you home after knowing you for five minutes. I like that kind of thing. I like the open nature of most Americans. Mark Savoy is a great accordion maker who runs a music store down in cajun country in Louisiana. Stores in America often have signs up saying 'No Dogs. No Shorts. No Sandals' in an attempt to keep up what they must see as some kind of standard.

Mark's store has a lovely sign. 'Dogs -no problem, Shorts - no problem, sandals - no problem. No Soul - stay away.' I like that man.

Hypnotising the Cat

Utah can sometimes be a problem for a man like myself. Being a Mormon state, a lot of hotels and restaurants are 'dry' ie. without alcohol. Suffering a case of near terminal thirst one Sunday night, I drove around the desert area near Zion National Park looking for a bar. As the light died I found a single-storey shack on the edge of nothing, a busted neon sign weakly flickering on the dusty night sky telling the world this was Truckers Heaven. I went in. The bar was full of men who made Giant Haystacks look like Jimmy Clitheroe. None of them had necks, their heads just sort of slid into their shoulders. A silence came on the room as I walked in, all pale and touristy and bespectacled. 'I'll take a beer,' I said in best Roy Rogers/Crumpsallese. A big man next to me stared at me as though I'd flown in on the eight o'clock UFO.

'Where you from buddy?'

'England.'

'Don't get too many folks from England round these parts.' I began to wonder whether I'd have to go and find a gun and meet him at high noon on the dusty road outside when I noticed an anti-nuclear poster behind the bar.

'What's that about?' I asked.

'The lady who used to run this place died of cancer of the thyroid. Only one way you get that kind o'cancer - strontium ninety. Only one way you get strontium ninety - fall-out from nuclear testing. We hate that crap!'

I don't suppose you'll doubt me when I tell you that it ended up with guitars and mouth-organs and I was very late back to my hotel.

● ●

I Married a Monster From Blackpool Outer Space

Roswell, New Mexico is the heart of UFO country. More people here have had close encounters of every kind than you can shake a stick at. Which is why the place has not just one but two UFO museums. In 1947 there was a mysterious aircraft crash on the hills just a few miles outside town. Something flying low had gone into the desert mountains and locals, thinking it was a plane from the nearby military airbase, phoned in to report an accident. The military came out and, according to local mythology, found a flying saucer and four dead aliens. A press officer at the air base gave out a press release in which he actually admitted that the military had taken a flying saucer and four space men to the Roswell base. Later he was forced to recant and claimed that it had all been a mistake and that what had come down was a weather balloon and there were no bodies at all and he hadn't been feeling well when he'd come out with all that nonsense about little green men. Of course it was too late by then and people began to suspect a cover-up and ever since there has been controversy over 'The Roswell Incident'. A few locals claimed to have seen the bodies being carried to a truck and the man who made the announcement later went back on his word again and said that it was all true and he'd been forced to counter his first statement. I don't have a clue what happened at Roswell in 1947 but I do know that people find it a lot more exciting to accept a conspiracy theory than that somebody just went off his tree for half an hour and made the whole thing up. Dozens of books have been written on the subject and Roswell is now the centre of UFOology which is why it has two museums devoted to the subject. I walked into the one on

Hypnotising the Cat

Main Street and wandered round looking at photographs of things that looked like Dutch caps and pudding basins shining over the desert and as I was reading something about a farmer from New Mexico who was taken up in a saucer by four men in silver suits, a lady in her seventies came up to me.

'Have you had your picture taken with Ralf?' she asked.

'Ralf?'

'That stands for Roswell Alien Life Form,' she said, - 'he's in here', and I followed her into a dimly lit room where a little creature about four foot tall with spindly limbs, a pear-drop head and big googly eyes was stood under a spotlight.

'Course he ain't real, he's just a model. But that's exactly what the bodies looked like they took from the crash. You go and stand by him. I'll take your picture.'

And I did. On the way out with my photograph of me and Ralf safely in my pocket, she asked me where I was from.

'England,' I said.

'I married one of them,' she replied.

Immediately I thought of Ralf.

'An alien?' I asked. In New Mexico anything is possible.

'Well sort of. He was a kind of alien. He was an Englishman from Blackpool called Akroyd. And she showed me her badge. 'Lorraine Akroyd', it said. So if any of you Blackpuddlians want to know what happened to Fred Akroyd late of Seaview House, Impetigo Terrace, Blackpool, he married a lady called Lorraine who takes pictures of people with Ralf in Roswell, New Mexico. Only in America could that happen.

I met a bloke in a bar last night and we got talking in the way you do in bars. People like to chat to find out about you and tell you a bit about themselves. Tommy was a builder who worked for himself building interesting architect-designed houses out in the hills. The great thing about the south-west is that there's so much space that people are very largely allowed to do their own thing. They build houses with towers and castle walls or build them like Mexican cantinas or ranches and nobody minds. It's all down to the individualism you find here; artists and writers have been coming here for years, ever since D.H. Lawrence and Georgia O' Keefe in the Twenties and Thirties, and it has produced a very special kind of artistic climate. There are probably more painters, writers and photographers here than in any other area of America. So I asked Tommy if he had a hobby, thinking he might paint or write.

'Sure. I go out in my pick-up truck with a six-pack and a chain saw and I cut down billboards, you know, those great big advertising things you see at the side of the road. Man I hate those things. They're making America look so goddam ugly!'

So, as I travel on towards Taos, Colorado and the Grand Canyon I will think of Tommy and The Utah Chain Saw Good Taste Massacre.

• •

Lady Chatterley's Adobe Hacienda

In most places in America you can get thirty-two televi sion channels. In The Sleepy Enchilada Motel, T a o s, New Mexico you can get sixty-seven and they are all absolute rubbish. There is one channel devoted entirely to shopping - they show you stuff and you phone a free-phone number and order it and it's delivered to you next morning. I didn't stay tuned long enough to see what the

commercials are, the news I guess. There is another channel that shows nothing but the weather, what it did, what
it's doing and what it might do. As you can imagine, it isn't
long before they're scraping round trying to find things to
say about the weather. They have weather for gardeners,
weather for anglers, weather for sail-boarders, weather
for jugglers - it's all the same weather but they're just
desperately trying to pad it out. Well, it takes about five
minutes to go through it, then they do it all again, then
there's a commercial break and they do it all again. It's like
having Michael Fish followed by Fish Fingers followed by
Michael Fish for twenty-four hours. There's another channel that is nothing but news. Any journalist with a professional, rolling-news axe to grind should watch this channel. After ten minutes you've seen it all. And because not
much has happened in the last ten minutes, they show it
you all again. This is the land of constant déjà déjà vu vu.

There's another channel that has Kilroy- and Oprah
Winfrey-type shows on all the time. People talk about
AIDS and divorce for three minutes, then there's a commercial break and they do it again, all before a studio
audience that presumably has to be drugged and dragged
into the studio. American television, in a word, represents
the end of civilisation as anybody knows it. It is popcorn
for the brain, tasteless, crass and bad for you. It represents
the end of thinking, the terminal death of the analytic
mind. You need the IQ of a garden snail to sit through
more than ten minutes of it.

And I'm afraid to say that British TV is going the
same way. You don't think so ? I remember being in
another motel room on the edge of the Monument Valley
Navajo Reservation a few years back watching a terrible,
terrible show with the audience whooping and shrieking
as people made total penis heads of themselves. Thank
God for the BBC, I thought, at least that crap will never get
on to British TV screens. The next year there it was beamed

out across England with our own Silly Black introducing it. *Blind Date* had made it across the pond following Big Macs, Coca Cola and *Roxanne*. And if Murdoch gets his way we'll be watching even more brainless dross and all in the name of choice. Well as far as I'm concerned digger, you can shove it where the kangaroo shoves its widgie grubs.

And another thing, since I'm feeling that way out this morning. It is virtually impossible to get a breakfast in America that is not going to either kill you on the spot or shorten your life by twelve hours per mouthful. Everything is fried, full of fat or covered with sugar. I ordered some French toast this morning in a diner called 'Cozee Cholesterol Corner' or 'From Here to Obesity' or some such; they can't do much with that, I thought. Not much they can't. It came to the table in the hands of a lady that made the Michelin Man look like Mahatma Gandhi. 'Enjoy,' she ordered, slamming down a plate of strips of toast that had been dipped in egg and deep fried, then coated with icing sugar. It was served up with a bowl of maple syrup to dip it in. I could feel the cholesterol racing along my arteries like formula-one slugs heading straight for the aorta. Why more people don't keel over and die in American restaurants I'll never understand. Every morning I expect some overweight trucker to groan and collapse head first into his eggs sunnyside up with ham and grits and blueberry pancakes and syrup, but they never do. They just waddle out to the truck and cruise off down the slab, probably exploding half-way down the road. 'Oh Oh!' the drivers say as they go past the mangled remains. 'Another trucker gone to the great health farm in the sky.'

D.H. Lawrence was a miner's son from Nottingham who wrote what some regard as among the finest novels and poetry in the English language. (I'm not talking about *Lady Chatterley*, I mean things like *Sons and Lovers* and *The*

Rainbow.) Lawrence spent some time in New Mexico living on a ranch north of Santa Fe, near Taos. He wrote and painted there and some of the crude art he produced is on show in one of the bars in town. You can see it for a dollar or so. When he died, his wife Freda brought his ashes back and placed them inside a shrine high on a hill at the end of a six-mile dirt track. I've been there twice now; a simple whitewashed chapel with an altar and a silver-painted phoenix looks out across the fir forests to the Taos plateau. Standing there as the evening light died across New Mexico this evening, I couldn't help wondering how many Pueblo Indians there are buried in Nottingham? An idle thought, but then again idle thoughts can be one of the less anti-social results of too much Mexican food. Not for nothing do they call the after-effects of too much chili 'Zapata's Revenge.'

• •

A Town Called ~~Alice, Eric, Jim,~~ The Ten O'Clock News

I t's a funny thing but all the American shows you see on TV in England (with the exception of *Roxanne*) show healthy, neat, good-looking, slim and healthy people. Stand on the edge of Monument Valley watching the coaches disgorge the trippers and you'll get a very different picture. The Americans you see there are often massively overweight and have spent so much time in their cars or as couch potatoes that they've forgotten what their legs are for. They don't walk, they sort of roll, like shell-suited amoeba. I like America, I really do, and the friends I have over here are wonderful, but sometimes looking round me I do fear for the future. It's possible now in most states of America to do everything you want without getting out of your car. They even have drive-in banks. They're like big petrol stations, only instead of petrol pumps they have pay stations. You put your cheque-book or credit card or whatever into a metal cylinder and drop it into a plastic tube. A blast of compressed air shoots it along the tube into the bank and a lady at the other end fires the money back at you. And that's it, you don't have to see or talk to anyone. Drive-in movies, drive-in hamburger and Pizza joints, drive-in washaterias, drive-in banks and drive-in churches. The churches - next to the supermarkets more buildings in America must be churches than anything else - Primitive Baptists, Methodists, Catholics, Snake-Handlers, the mountains are full of them. Seven million people in North Carolina and four million of them are Baptists. If they carry on this way perhaps Americans will start to evolve into a legless life form that passes its life spending, eating and praying. Who knows - watch this space.

On the way to the Grand Canyon a few days back I passed through Tuba City. I like the name. Tuba City - it's like calling somewhere Saxophone Super Mare or Euphonium on Crouch. Americans are pretty good at giving their towns strange names, it's a kind of folk art. There's a place in Pennsylvania called Intercourse and another small town close by called Paradise. It goes almost without saying that there is a well-photographed signpost bearing the legend 'Intercourse to Paradise'. There's a town I drove through in New Mexico called Truth or Consequence. It's called that because a game show of that name advertised a prize of several thousand dollars for the first town that would be prepared to change its name to Truth or Consequence. And the small town in New Mexico took the money and changed. I heard somewhere that the original name was Crap-Head City and that nobody was too upset about the new name but I'm not sure if I believe that.

Still, Truth or Consequence does make me wonder if Cleckheaton fancies changing its name to Blankety Blank or Leamington Spa to Busman's Holiday? The mind almost boggles. I'm sure if there was enough money in it Basildon would become Blind Date.

The friend I'm staying with here in Scaly Mountain, North Carolina, is the poet and photographer Jonathan Williams, who spends six months in the Smoky Mountains and six months as my neighbour in the Yorkshire Dales. He's a great collector of folk art and curious bits and pieces, author of books of poetry like *Get Hot Or Get Out* and collections of odd bits of unconsidered trifles and ephemera such as the following from a church wall in Stalingfleet Church, North Yorkshire; 'Without the friendship of the Happy dead how should we bear our life?' He heard me talking about Tuba City and showed me a collection of American place names he's picked up over the years. The list is too long to print in full but here's a selection. These are all the names of real towns in America - Possum Trot - Ordinary - Skullbuster - Pig - Chicken Bristle - Araminta Ward's Bottom - Boring - Rabbit Hash-and my favourite, Monkey's Eyebrow.

Travelling along the long, seemingly endless roads of Utah the other day I overtook an RV. RV stands for Recreational Vehicle and they are basically enormous motor homes. America caters for RVs brilliantly. You can pull into RV parks with full 'hook-up' and in five minutes you are on mains sewage, electricity and water. I travelled from Las Vegas out across Death Valley in one five years ago with the fridge stocked full of Mexican beer in case I broke down. At least I wouldn't die of thirst; 'Highway patrol to base. We've found him Captain. He's been twelve days lost in the deserts of Death Valley. He's still alive but he won't come in unless he can bring the purple elephant and the green and pink crocodile with him.' The RV is a good way to see America and in fact a lot of Americans coming up to retirement age simply sell up and buy one and spend their last years travelling, just seeing America. But what impressed me was that the RV I passed this morning was being driven by a guy who must have been in his eighties. There was a motorbike clamped on the front and a sign on the back that read:

Too old to work - Too young to die
Just cruising the road - Bye bye.

Only in America.

• •

A Letter from Toronto

I read a piece in an in-flight magazine on the way here from North Carolina that described how Gary Kasparov beat a chess computer. It wasn't any run of the mill kid's stuff games computer either - it was the world's champion chess computer, one of the most powerful computers ever devised, the magazine said - and Kasparov beat it. On the following page there was an article on airline safety that told you how most of the world's great aircraft are really flown not by the pilots but by computers. Now hang on a minute, if computers are more stupid than humans then what the hell are we doing letting them fly airplanes? Since I was sat in seat 25B of an American Airlines Boeing 737 when I read this, I was not a happy camper.

Hypnotising the Cat

I saw a gang of boys on a Toronto street last night. They were wearing baseball caps on back to front, baggy check shirts and long shorts that came below their knees. They were chewing gum and talking loudly and carrying skateboards under their arms, looking for somewhere to use them. They must have been fourteen years old on average, I suppose. It struck me then that I had seen the same gang of kids somewhere before. It was in Nashville, and Salt Lake City, London, Manchester and Cleethorpes. Were they following me round the world? Was this some kind of conspiracy or was I, like the Prisoner, trapped in some kind of global Portmerion, being followed by these weird skateboarding kids who are after my immortal soul? Then I realised they weren't the same kids at all, they were just kids who were the same. They were archetypal universal, Platonist thingy, Coca-Cola-drinking, Big Mac-eating, MTV-watching, gum-chewing, skateboarding, baseball-cap-wearing kids.

It also struck me that they live in a world apart, of which I have no knowledge. We have nothing in common beyond a shared dislike of ballroom dancing and the fact that I wrote the music for *Dangermouse* and they might have seen it when they were little. I find myself on the wrong side of the barricades and I don't like it.

I feel estranged, cut off somehow, consigned to the world of the 'square' and 'un-cool', the ghetto of the boring old farts. I didn't watch *Wayne's World* and don't know who Curt Cobain was and I've never managed more than two minutes of Nintendo Super Whatsit Thingy. I can't stand McDonalds or Coke and think Beavis and Butthead are pathetic. But perhaps it's me that's wrong. Maybe I should turn up tomorrow in Albert Square with a skateboard, long shorts and a baseball cap on back to front and hang out with the guys. Do you think they'd notice?

147

Hypnotising the Cat

I'm in Toronto on the last leg of the tour of North America. I've got relatives here, my cousins George and Pat and Maire emigrated here from Besses o'th' Barn in the Fifties and Uncle Bobby and Aunty Kitty followed in the Sixties. Aunty Kitty is dead now but Uncle Bobby is a fit and bright ninety-five who still argues politics with the same passion he did when I was a nipper. He was a tailor at Springfield Hospital, Crumpsall for thirty-some years and was a big union man. I remember him most of all because he was a star. He took me walking and fishing and gave me some of the best times of my childhood. Growing up in Crumpsall wasn't exactly a rural experience - the first time I saw a cow I thought it was a black and white bus. We couldn't afford to go away for holidays so I used to go all the way to Besses for weeks at a time in the summer and that old electric Manchester to Bury line was a way out into another world for me. Crumpsall, Bowker Vale, Heaton Park, Prestwich, Besses o' th' Barn, I would count the stations off, my nose pressed to the glass, a little boy off to have adventures, Crumpsall's answer to Huckleberry Finn. Once there, as far as I was concerned, I was in the real country. Never mind that there was a golf course and a mental hospital on either side, there were hedgehogs and wild flowers and fish in the ponds and Uncle Bobby took me out for long walks with Vic the dog. He doesn't do any long walking now, he brews his own beer and watches ice-hockey, cheering on every team but the Toronto Maple Leafs and tonight, as I sit in the Salutation back in Manchester with my first real pint in five weeks in front of me, I will think of him watching the match and raise my glass in salute. May every small child in the world have somebody like him, cheers Uncle Bobby.

• •

Shall I Compare Thee to an Ozone Smog?

So that was summer then, was it? I'd just taken off the woolly vest that I'd been sewn into at the beginning of winter, burned the brown paper and goose grease that had saved me from croup and scrofula and ironed the shorts ready for the legs' first airing in the daylight, when the weather turned all cold and nasty again. Sleet and frost and the usual grey murky skies. Just what you expect at the end of May. Like Frank Sinatra, Winter is making yet another comeback. Ah well, it's being so cheerful keeps me going. But they truly are getting very short the summers nowadays. I remember when a summer used to last at least four weeks. What did we get this year - eight days. It was hot and sunny and lewd did sing the cuckoo, when he wasn't choking with the ozone-induced asthma that is. And then that was it. After singing lewd, the cuckoo naffed off again to Spain or Weymouth or wherever it is cuckoos go in the winter. And it's no use putting up barbed wire to keep the cuckoo in so that it'll be summer all year round like they did near Oldham once. Cuckoos are very clever and can pole-vault over barbed wire.

But that's it, that's the heat wave for another year. Probably a good job anyway since I have one of those noses that falls off in the sun. The rest of me goes an interesting shade of mud, but the nose just peels off, 'sloughs' I think the *mot juste* is. It sloughs repeatedly like a hyperactive snake and I end up with a pink beezer such as the Dong with the Luminous Snozzer would have been proud of.

But even when it was hot you couldn't go out in case you choked to death with the summer smogs. The government who advised us all to stay indoors with wet towels over our mouths will tell us it's not their fault that one in seven schoolchildren and one in three cuckoos have to have ventilators for their asthma, and it's not their fault that, just when it's hottest and sunniest and the great outdoors beckons most tantillatingly, we're being told to stay in because for the first time in the history of this planet breathing may kill you or seriously damage your health. This government, which dropped to its knees and began licking the exhaust pipes of passing cars and building motorways like they were going out of fashion (which they are) when She Who Had To Be Obeyed, the Ghastly Ga Ga Grannie of Grantham, told us she believed in a car-owning democracy, now tell us that it's not their fault, it's the foreigners again. We should have known, it's all that Common Market's fault. Our own twenty million vehicles emit essence of roses, so pure that new-born babies could and should breathe it for the sake of their health. Our air is fine, it's the Frogs and the Krauts again sending their filth over here that's the problem. At least that is what one government transport spokesman told us last week. All this smog in our cities is stuff that's being blown across from the continent. Just a minute, I may be stupid but I'm not thick. When I was at school we were taught that the winds that crossed Britain were prevailing westerlies; Europe is east and south of us, in that case there has been a new development and there is now a new type of wind that sucks. I suppose it's just another case of the government's message failing to get across and that if we'd only have listened hard enough we would have understood. We got the smell from Europe's muck-spreading a few days back and now they're sending us their petro-chemical air. It's what comes of being in the Common Market I suppose. We send them our football psychopaths and they send us their smog and the reek from their dung - it's a fair swap. It just seems a shame that never again will a Swan of Avon be able to ask:

Shall I compare thee to a summer's day?
Thou art more lovely and more temperate.
Rough winds do shake the darling buds of May ...

No they don't, mate, the buds have all fallen off in the
chemical soup we're all trying to breathe.

● ●

Lost Accountant Found in Condom!

There is a game played amongst the chattering classes
of Crumpsall and around the dinner tables of Ancoats
after the port has been passed from right to leftand
the *Romeo et Juliets* are being warmed over the flames. For
this game you have to imagine that you're in the basket of
a hot air balloon with world-important figures like the
Pope, Mother Theresa, Tolstoy, William Shakespeare,
George Best, Nobby Carr etc. and suddenly the balloon
springs a leak. Ditching one person can save the lives of all
the others and you have to decide which person least
deserves to stay in the basket. So now it's out - According
to a recent book Mark Thatcher really is the kind of man
most of the population of this country would have no
trouble giving sudden un-aided flying lessons to. The
book draws a picture of him as a thick and nasty spoilt
monster who became a millionaire in ways perhaps not
unconnected with his mummy's apron strings.

I will say one small thing on this subject and then I
will be as shtum as the six foot of earth duvet in case the
Thought Police decide to drag me off to the Eccles Lubianka.

Hypnotising the Cat

If the book is correct and Mark Thatcher is a sometime accountant and part-time racing driver who trotted around the world in the shadow of the Mad Gran of Grantham, and if Little Mark is an intellectually challenged, spoilt child that nobody likes very much, then we should do what this lot of second-hand Victorian morality salesmen that we call a government are always telling us to do and blame the parents. Since Mummy always seemed the stronger of the two and Daddy was often away playing golf and making millions, then I think we should 'Cherchez la femme', as they say in Ecclefechan. I rest my case.

As a parting squib, a few years back I was on a comedy tour around the country when it was announced that Mark Thatcher had got himself lost in the Sahara Desert on the Paris-Dacca rally. Since he was sponsored by Durex at the time I ad-libbed into the microphone something to the effect that Durex was a product his father should have sponsored thirty-odd years before. There was a silence you could have knocked nails in and then I recollected that Guildford, on whose famous stage I was stood, was hardly a hotbed of Marxist-Leninist Anarcho-Syndicalists. Aye well, you win some and you lose a lot.

● ●

Hypnotising the Cat

Open Wide Lie Back and Think of Gnnnghangia

I went to see my dentist the other morning, a sterling chap who has looked after my peggies for a long time and over the years has become a good friend. Vic and I have dined together, supped excellent single malts together and even discussed at short length the merits of Manchester City Football Team. But what is it with dentists? I know several of them and though they are all extremely fine people, pillars of the community, good fathers and all that, they are each and every one of them, without doubt or contradiction, a boy scout short of a jamboree.

You arrive at the surgery and sit in the waiting room reading ten-year-old copies of *Punch, Lancashire Life* and *Classic Car* while the fish in the fish tank he bought to relax his patients slowly die and rise belly up to float on the tepid surface. From down the corridor come muffled groans and whimpers and the sound of somebody moving a very heavy wardrobe over cobbles on their own. Then he appears at the waiting room door sweating, gory and grim, the veins on his biceps pulsing like a knot of mating earthworms. 'Next!!' he screams, while behind him the nurse helps something to the door that looks like Quasimodo after a tram smash.

'Just get on the chair and relax,' he says and you lie back while he shines a very bright light in your eyes and does extremely painful things to you with sharp instruments while telling you at the same time that it isn't hurting. As a kind of foreplay he shoves an anaesthetic syringe with a needle the size of a telegraph pole into your upper gum and keeps on shoving. When I was small and the chimney-sweep came to our house we used to run out into the street and watch the chimney-pot to tell him when the brush appeared. The dentist has a nurse to tell him when the needle has come into sight out of the top of your head. She gets sixpence every time.

Then when the anaesthetic has taken effect and it feels as though somebody has stuck an extra four inches of dead and frozen meat on the front of your face, he fills your mouth with two and a half hundredweight of clamps, pumps, water sprays, drains, suckers and gauze pads and while all this is sucking, pumping and whirring away he introduces the drill to your tooth and just at the moment that the smoke from your burning dentine starts to drift across the surgery he asks you where you are going for your holidays.

'Gnnnghanghia,' you answer.

'That's funny,' he says deadly serious. 'You know - a lot of my patients go there.'

I wonder if dentists really do believe that there is a holiday resort called Gnnnghangia that is extremely popular with their patients? I picture them late at night, a balloon of brandy in their hand, searching the atlas for the tropical island muttering, 'It must be here somewhere. They're all going there this year.'

• •

With This Half a Fridge I Thee Do Cherish

I went to a wedding the other day. I don't normally like weddings, I much prefer funerals. At least you know how a funeral is going to turn out; half the time now you go to weddings and they split up at the reception and start arguing about who gets possession of the cake and the wedding album before they've got to the telegrams. It's wiser buying wedding presents in pairs nowadays; that way, when they split up they get one each. There's nothing worse than watching a couple sawing a fridge in two or taking the axe to a Goblin Teasmaid, and you can't cut a duvet in half without getting feathers all over the place.

This wedding was different though and I really enjoyed it. One of my daughter's old school friends was marrying the man of her dreams and a jolly affair it was too. The church was a Catholic church made from a converted cinema and the two priests who took the ceremony in tandem were more like Abbot and Costello than Abbot and Bishop. In fact one of them told a few good jokes that wouldn't have been out of place in the *Gang Show*. Here's one of them.

'Now it's quite normal for the bride to be late to church, that's her privilege,' he told us all from what used to be the altar but was now a sort of stage. 'But for the priest to be late for a wedding is something else. Well, there was one wedding in this church a few years back and the priest was very late getting to the church, the sail had fallen off his car or his bicycle had melted or something. He was a good few hours late. In fact he was so late the bride was just starting labour and some of the altar boys had grown moustaches. ('That wasn't really true I made that bit up to help the story along,'he added) Anyway when he got to the church they were all waiting for him and he apologised and got on with the job and no harm taken.

Ten years later the priest saw your man in the street. "I bet you don't remember that fright I gave you ten years ago?" he said.

"Yes I do," said your man, "I'm still married to her."

There were lots more jokes in a similar vein and once people realised they were allowed to laugh in church it got to be a jolly do. While the couple signed the register a short sighted tubby bloke got on stage (sorry - the altar) and played guitar while a minute lady sang *Stand By Me* and the audience banged tambourines and rattled tins of dried peas and such stuff by way of accompaniment.

All of this of course is a long, long way away from when I was an altar boy when the whole thing was very solemn and in Latin and a full nuptial mass like this one would have had at least six altar boys and a couple of priests. Nuptial masses were always popular with us altar boys because we usually got good tips - ten bob each on average - and it was popular with the priests because they usually got invited back to the reception where there was lots of free booze and good food. But the ceremony itself was much more serious then with the priest keeping his back to the audience so they couldn't see what was up his sleeve, and the altar rail represented a no man's land beyond which the audience (sorry, congregation) were not allowed. And the host was absolutely sacred (no pun intended), you were never allowed to touch it with your teeth or fingers. The priest put it in your mouth and that was that; you were forbidden to lick it or chew it and were expected somehow to get it to the back of your throat and swallow it. Getting that dry wafer past the roof of your mouth and past your tonsils and that little bit of doodah hanging down like a stalagtite, the Ursula or whatever they call it, was a dreadful business. I've no idea how many heart-stopping Sunday mornings I knelt with my tongue half-way up the back of my nostrils trying to get the body of the Son of God off the roof of my mouth. Now they give it you in your hand! Lord bless us and save us, before too long they'll be giving you butter and a choice of marmite and honey with it!

Talking about weddings - here's a silly altar boy story I heard from Marilyn Monroe when we were on a cruise together. A visiting priest who wouldn't have looked

Hypnotising the Cat

out of place in *Snow White and the Seven Priests* came to Marilyn's parish. To be politically correct, he was what is known as vertically challenged - so much so that he had to stand on a crate of Guinness so that he could be seen over the top of the pulpit. One Saturday night after confession Father Riprap, the parish priest, convinced that the visiting curate was drinking secretly, took the crate back to the off licence and got the money back on it. The next morning at mass the curate had nothing to stand on and when he climbed the pulpit to read the gospels all people could see were the tips of his fingers wiggling like a sea anemone on speed or Punch and Judy in the nude.

'I am the light of the world!' he cried.

And a recovering drunk at the back shouted:

'Well turn your wick up - we can't see you!'

I am often warmed by stories that I hear along the way and in the Yorkshire Dales the other night I heard a story that cheered me greatly. There's a carpet fitter lives close by to a friend of mine - five feet ten, built like a concrete urinal, muscles in his spit, tattoos, shaved head and a tiny pigtail - all the accoutrements that would lead one to suspect a thuggish nature. Wrong. He is sweet as a pea and has a passion for wildlife and all things natural. He's a bird-watcher, badger-watcher and wild-flower fanatic. He lives on a country lane where drivers regularly run over hedge-hogs - and many times it would seem that they do it on purpose. So when he finds a dead hedgehog he skins it, wraps the pelt round a brick and leaves it in the road. Along comes a driver, sees the hedgehog and thinks, 'Ey up! Must be my birthday! - sitting target!!' So he aims for the hedgehog - hits the brick, bursts tyre, dents rim etc etc. It cheered my day up greatly did that story.

●●●●●●●●●●●●●●●●●●●●●●●

It's A Long Road That Has no Turnips

I came across an old Irish proverb the other day - '*I dtir na ndall is rí fear na leathshúile*', which you will already know means, 'In the land of the blind the one-eyed man is king.' It struck me then how many old saws and proverbs carry within them seeds of not just great wisdom but seeds of absolutely mind-numbing nonsense too. If everybody in that land was blind then they wouldn't know that this bloke who called himself the king could see, would they? It's a bit like saying, 'In the valley of the deaf the lady saxophone player is queen.' If you couldn't hear her you wouldn't give a chuff whether she could play the saxophone or not. You'd just turn to your mate and sign, 'Why is that woman sucking a long brass tube with bits on?' It's like that other saying, 'Many a mickle makes a muckle.' I wouldn't know a muckle maker if I trod on one! And unless there's a family called 'Mickle' and they all make muckles then I can't see any sense in the saying at all. 'It's a long road that has no turnings.' Really? Is it? Well I suppose it is. It's a long road and it has no turnings - how interesting. I suppose if it was a short road with a turning or two or a cul de sac we'd have nothing to say about it at all.

'In vino veritas.' Absolute rubbish! In vino gibberish is more like it. Have you ever tried to hold a conversation with a drunk when you are sober? You'll get a better class of conversation out of a garden snail.

I must tell you that my world fell apart this morning. I went down for the post, hung-over and unshaven, garbed only in my silk peignoir, fending off the amorous advances of Zoroaster the dog, who has fallen in love with my leg again, and as I made my way back towards the kitchen and the first cup of tea of the day, I opened one of the envelopes and was immediately halted in my tracks. The dog, taking advantage of my immobility, began acting out scenes from *Hot Dutch* on my lower limb, without any foreplay, sweet nothings or candlelit dinner. The envelope contained an anonymous letter forwarded by the *Manchester Evening News*, upon which worthy journal I am a columnist, and the letter was a piece of what I've come to know and love as Barmpot Mail. I get occasional nice letters from people who find I've touched a chord. I get a lot more from people whose whole world view has been endangered by my usually harmless gibberings.

I don't regard myself as an intellectual or an expert on anything much unless it's Manchester Irish tenor banjo players circa 1989. As a philosopher I rank alongside the late Arnold Parrot, Barnsley Lighthouse Keeper and *bon viveur*, who once remarked, 'If we weren't here we'd be somewhere else' - as nice a piece of existential rhetoric as you'd ever wish to meet on a dark night.

So all I am is a jobbing columnist and I'm a bit of a dead loss at that really since I just burble along about anything that comes into my head in what I think is a generally inoffensive way. But this letter was from someone who believes in flying saucers and got upset when I said I didn't in an article I wrote on a trip I had made to America, where there are only three people in the entire country who haven't been either abducted by aliens, sexually interfered with by aliens or had aliens looking in their front room windows making snide comments on the soft furnishings.

I don't know if you've been following the reports, but to be serious for a nano-second, all over America (and to a lesser extent in this country too) people are claiming that they have been taken up into spaceships by aliens. The reports all follow a similar pattern; the abductees see bright lights in the sky, a saucer-like object lands and silver-clad beings come out of the craft. The people feel powerless, they are taken up in the craft and once there they are usually subjected to some kind of sexual experimentation. Then they wake up, usually in bed, feeling all hot and bothered and they phone the police and report it. And the police, instead of remarking calmly, 'Madam, you are barking mad', take them seriously and get psychiatrists from the local university to look at them and the psychiatrists take them seriously and write books about it which sell serious amounts and make serious money. Now I have one point to make here. Before the hi-tech age we are living in, people reported that they were abducted by demons, hob-goblins, fairies and witches and they were either smoking serious quantities of henbane or they were barking mad too. Now that we live in a hi-tech age, the wizened crone with the wart on the end of her nose and the leprechaun with the red cap and the shoe-maker's hammer have been replaced by little, spindly-legged, egg-headed, silver-painted aliens that take our women into space and do rude things with them.

I suppose kids don't play doctors and nurses nowadays, they play aliens and abductees instead. 'I am Smorg from the planet Transpontania - get your knickers off while I look at you. ' Quite a few of the barmpots who claim to have been up in these flying IVF clinics report that there is some sort of crêche in outer space where alien/human baby cross-breeds are being nurtured. This is presumably all part of some plan for a new world order and is some kind of plot hatched by the UN, the Elders of Zion, Noddy and Big Ears and Muffin the Mule. This would all be laughable and of no consequence were it not for the fact that, since most of this UFO stuff goes on in America, a lot of these people have guns and if there's anything worse than a barking mad nutter, it's a barking mad nutter with a gun.

Hypnotising the Cat

Serves You Right for Having One

The car got done over again the other night. I didn't expect the pond-life that make a living out of petty crime would have bothered scaling the compound fence of the car park I'd left it in under the nose of the security guards to smash three cars up and pinch the radios, but they did. I wouldn't mind if it was a particularly good radio but it was that old it still got Hilversum and Henry Hall. But they smashed the window and offed it. This particular car has been so regularly looted that I've lost count. One bright summer's day the car was parked on the main road near a bus stop in full view. No problem, they smashed the window and offed a leather jacket and a Sony Walkman. Another time they broke the window, got in and wrecked the dashboard trying to get the radio out. I got in the car to drive it to the garage and the steering wheel came off in my hand at the first bend, they'd broken that too trying to start the car. It was like one of those old Keystone Kops movies, the car swerving all over the road and me staring at the steering wheel in my hands wondering what to do.

I don't drive a posh car; cars to me are tools for getting from A to somewhere else in the alphabet and all I have is a six-year-old jeep-type thing that I am going to keep until it falls apart, since I refuse to pay the price of a decent cottage in Clare for a lot of Japanese ironmongery. So I don't have any sentimental regard for cars. But what really pigs me off is having to fill in claims forms and spend hours on the phone trying to find a glass replacement company that has a quarter light for a six-year-old Nagahumamichi short wheelbase Tojo - this time I had to drive to Carnforth beyond Lancaster just to get the window replaced.

Hypnotising the Cat

Now I don't want to sound like Mr. Angry and I know my story isn't unique (in fact I don't know anybody who hasn't been burgled) but there is a point to this story.

The long-haired person who shares the house with me has a very good brain and she was so angry at being woken again in the middle of the night by nice policeman who have visited us so many times that they have squatters' rights on our kitchen, telling us that the car was now full of glass and cut wires, that in a flash of inspiration while stood there in her dressing gown making tea for the constables, she single-handedly came up with the solution to the nation's crime wave. 'Most crime is carried out by young men between the ages of fifteen and thirty,' she said, 'so all we have to do is lock all men up when they get to fifteen and don't let them out again until they're thirty-one. While they're inside we should ban weightlifting and all that nonsense and teach them cake decoration, bobbin work and macramé.'

'I think it's too much testosterone,' I said.

'I wouldn't let the shops sell it to them,' she answered and that was the end of that.

I did wonder whether putting bromide in young men's tea would make a difference or perhaps we should bring back the stocks and put them up in the shopping mall and lock offenders up in them all day Saturday so the rest of us can go and throw rotten eggs and tomatoes at them. Hard men don't like looking silly and you can't look hard covered in egg yolk and pips.

Some of you out there will be tut-tutting saying, 'But we have to understand the causes of crime'. As a self-confessed liberal I do understand the causes and I feel very sorry for the poor young men who have to go out night after night burgling and mugging. It must be awful for them. I bet they cut their hands sometimes on the glass and they probably get quite dirty climbing over garden walls. I bet it's cold too in winter, and it rains occasionally so they probably get wet sometimes. It's very sad for them. There's probably a glut on the market anyway with all the car radios and videos that have been stolen in the last ten years, so the poor thieves probably have a really hard time flogging them.

Who buys the stuff anyway? I've never been offered a car radio or a video in a pub - and I drink in some pretty hairy places at times - where does the stuff all go to? Here's a thought - perhaps the burglars are employed by the video and radio manufacturers and they steal our stuff so we have to go and buy more. Then again I suppose it's just all part of living in Post Thatcher (doesn't all that seem a long time ago?) Britain.

•••••••••••••••••••••

God is A White Anglo Saxon Chelsea Supporter

Have you ever wondered what happened to Mr. Pastry? In those short-trousered days in the blue remembered hills of Crumpsall, those days of gob stoppers and love hearts, donkey stones and dolly blue, Mr. Pastry was the Mr. Bean and Jacques Tati of the airwaves of the day. We in Harding Towers had no television, but the old lady next door, Mrs. Whitaker and her son Stan who had fought in the Desert Rats, had one of the first televisions in the street. The cabinet was the size of a small wardrobe but, like most of the televisions of the day, it only had a nine-inch screen, so some enterprising spark had invented a magnifier that hung over the front, filled with water and held on by thick leather straps. It looked like some kind of torture instrument and distorted every-thing at the edges so that when the cowboys and Indians chased each other across Monument Valley the horses had legs that were eighteen feet long and the wheels of the covered wagons were egg-shaped. It was of course black and white, and the picture quality was poor, compared to today's wide screen truer-than-life colour goggle boxes. The picture was mainly shades of grey and blurred at that - coupled with the distorting magnifier this made watch-ing it like being on drugs without any of the side effects. Mrs. Whitaker was a lovely lady and thought nothing of letting half the kids in the street sit cross-legged on her carpet watching *Children's Hour*.

There was never any fighting or pinching or shout-ing. We sat there turned to stone, staring wordlessly at the grey fuzzy murk, captivated by the oracle of Crystal Pal-ace. It must have looked like one of those old engravings you used to see in Victorian biographies of British mis-sionaries in Africa, open-mouthed natives jumping back in amazement at the projected image of a lion on a screen with the caption underneath telling us that we are looking at 'Fuzzy Wuzzies Captivated by the Reverend Mungo Shufflewick's Magic Lantern Show in the Bush'. In truth we were as hooked as a gaggle of Matabele. At five o'clock the street would empty, the 'rallevo' and 'kick-can' forgot-ten and we would pile into Mrs. Whittaker's to squat cross-legged on the rag rug. The curtains would be drawn and then, after some rings had gone round a pylon, Patricia Driscoll would talk to us in an accent that sounded like Martian but we knew was really the Queen's English. Then, after Muffin the Mule had done not very much on the piano lid again, Mr. Pastry would come on with his glasses and wild grey hair to cheers of delight from the Crumpsall Critics and, I assume, from various other gangs sat in darkened rooms throughout the land. He didn't do much, most of his gags centred round him decorating a room or whitewashing a wall and ended with him covered in paste with his foot in the bucket or stranded in a featureless box of a room with a papered-over door. Everything he did turned into dross and he staggered from one calamity to another with that Middle English Buffer's air that is quite endearing and yet infuriating at the same time. Now I remember what happened to Mr. Pastry. He's had a haircut, got some new glasses, called himself John and he's running the country.

Talking of Matabeles, I manage to steer clear of racists most of the time but I got one the other night, a classic - and drunk to boot. I think he must have mistaken me for that other well-known North Manchester comedian because he definitely saw me as a fellow spirit. I was in a pub having a quiet drop of the stuff when I saw him navigating his way between the tables like a sinking ship seeking landfall in the fog along a rocky coast. He had a face like a well-smacked backside and the kind of eyes that signify that all the lights are on but there's nobody at home. He was, I would have guessed, in middle management, in his thirties and well suited, hardly the kind whose hearth and home would be endangered by imagined hordes of immigrants wanting his job.

'Too many bloody immigrants in this country,' he led off with, 'Too many bloody Pakis', which you must admit is not bad for starters.

Now when I hear this kind of doo doo I have to be very careful. I am not a skilled debater but if my wits are about me I can occasionally wrong-foot even a sober opponent by my surrealist arguments. It is not for nothing that I am known as the Salvador Dali of the *mot juste*.

'I'm more worried about the Eskimos,' I countered. He stared at me, his eyes flickering with what passed for life, like a watchman's brazier seen from a distance on a cold, wet windy night.

'Eskimos?'

'They're coming over here in their thousands taking all the jobs in the ice cream factories, working in the frozen food cold stores, all that kind of stuff. They don't mind the cold, see, and they're cheap to employ - bit of blubber, a few candles now and then. And of course once you let one lot in, they get all their friends and relations in too. Manchester Ship Canal's thick with kayaks some days. But while we're on about immigrants what's your name?'

'Henderson.'

'Interesting name that,' I said. 'Viking name originally, they were among our most interesting early immigrants. But where most Pakistani immigrants content themselves with opening good restaurants, running clothing factories or working as surgeons in our major hospitals, the Vikings sacked monasteries, melted down beautiful gold ornaments, burnt about fifty editions of the Book of Kells and murdered, raped and looted their way round before settling down to raise families whose ancestors would get jobs in middle management. Interesting pedigree you've got.'

He stared at me dimly, the idea that I might be extracting the urine just beginning to present itself at the door of his mind like a Jehovah's Witness on a foggy night.

'In any case all the Asians that I know are hard-working people with a great sense of family and community. They look after their old people and generally appear in court far less than your average white male youth.'

He floundered a bit at this and, sensing he was out of his depth now, I went for the jugular.

'In any case, as the descendant of murdering, iconoclast rapists, can you tell me how many Pakistani burglars you know?'

● ●

Hypnotising the Cat

Britain's First Bean Assisted Man In Space

If I could make stuff up as funny as some of the things I've come across in my short sojourn on the skin of this cosmic apple spinning through the great greengrocer's shop of eternity, then believe me I would. I open the paper this morning and what do I read? That the news on BBC Radio Wales is to be read by a gentleman called Owen Money; we must be thankful that he isn't reading the financial reports. In Australia a few years back I heard of a couple called Carter who called their son Orson only to have that piece of information eclipsed by learning about a Mr. and Mrs. Christmas who called their son Murray. It makes being called Michael, Christopher, Damien Harding seem quite sensible even though Damien was the patron saint of lepers, French polishers and hub-cap dint removers.

As if Owen Money wasn't enough for one day, I turned the radio on this afternoon to hear a news report on the European bean mountain which is now apparently a few million tonnes. This was immediately followed, without any sense of the ludicrous, by a short piece on an Olympic long-jumper whose record long-jump was discounted because he was, and I quote, 'wind assisted'. Thoughts of long-jumpers and high-jumpers (not to mention hop, skip and jump-jumpers) being disqualified for secret bean eating flashed across my mind, only to be eclipsed by the image of a bean-eating, jet-assisted pole-vaulter ending up in low-level orbit - but then again I always did have a cartoonist's imagination.

At one time I used to collect strange newspaper headlines but after a time the house grew too small. 'No Water So Firemen Improvised' ran a close second to a wartime header, 'Eighth Army Push Bottles Up Germans' in my all-time collection of favourite barking weird headlines. Now lost in the great paper shredder of Time is the headline from the *News of the World* that, if I remember right, went something like 'Nude Chinese Laundry Worker and Wife of Circus Knife Thrower in Kinky Sex Romp with Co-op Pig Farm Manager'. You couldn't make stuff like that up if you tried. However, I digress.

I don't want you to think that I am anally fixated, but the other day I saw a tee-shirt stretched across the quivering torso of an anorexically challenged gentleman who was walking down the street towards me eating a Big Mac. On his cropped head was a baseball cap back to front while behind him trailed a lady also eating a Big Mac and similarly dressed, to whom were attached two small Big-Mac-eating whining children who seemed to be called 'Bleedin' Sean' and 'Bleedin' Joeleen.' The shirt was a simple white affair with three words blazoned on the front that puzzled me at first. 'Pull My Finger', it said. That was all. I pondered this for a while as the bulbous wearer of the shirt and his attendant tribe wobbled off into the city summer smog full of e-numbers and cholesterol. Then like St Paul on the road to Cleckheaton it hit me in a blinding flash: 'PULL MY FINGER' - of course it was every father and uncle's favourite trick. 'Pull my finger', they would say to you and when you did tug on the digit, as though by magic they would produce what medical specialists call 'a botty cough'. For years I thought this was a piece of true magic and nearly dislocated my Uncle Harry's fingers trying to elicit repeat trouser barks out of him one night. The poor man had arrived back from the Cleveland with too much Holt's Bitter in him than was good for a man in his condition, well, anybody in any condition actually. I have a theory that Holt's Bitter, much as I like it, is probably second only to high-octane aviation fuel in its propellant qualities. Come to think of it, a combination of

Holt's and beans would ensure the England athletics squad several golds at the next Olympics. However, I digress.

What I really wanted to talk about is the lack of any manners among old people nowadays. I don't know what they teach old people in this day and age but they certainly don't teach them how to behave. I'm fed up with old ladies ramming overloaded tartan shopping trolleys into me in the street and shoving me out of the way in check-out queues at Sainsbury's. And as for elderly gents with walking sticks getting on the bus - well I have a collection of deep purple scars to show the effect of a whack from a stout blackthorn on the human shinbone. And as if physical abuse wasn't bad enough, the verbal assault on the ears can be terrifying! Once they start on about the War you've as much chance of stopping them as you have of seeing the Norfolk Mountain Rescue Team in action. I've seen the glazed look spreading across the eyes of many a poor victim as, clutched by the hand of an Ancient Mariner soundalike, every detail of Basic Training Fulwood Barracks November to January 1941 was gone through, only to be followed by the NAAFI price lists from Wadi El Sup North Africa and the effects of the Manchester Blitz on the price of birds from the Pigeon Market in Shudehill. I've nothing against old people, with the help of God and a few policemen I'll get there myself one day, but they certainly aren't as well behaved as they used to be and something should be done about it.

All of which reminds me of the story of the Texan driving through Lancashire who stops his hire-car just outside Oswaldtwistle where an old timer is leaning over the gate. After a few minutes' banter about the weather and the weather, the Texan asks, 'Have you lived here all your life?'

There is a moment's pause and the farmer drily replies,

'Not yet I haven't'.

Gay (No Scene) Sergeant Pepper WLTM, NS, GSOH

I'd never really understood the power of the press until recently when I started reading the Lonely Hearts and Agony Columns of a national newspaper. I had always thought that, in the main, newspapers did just as their name described - they told the news and they were made of paper and that, as far as I was concerned, was that. The news can be anything from another lost fax making its way to Jonathan Aitken to a grandmother in Eccles who has learnt sword swallowing so that she can raise money for charity. All of this is grist to the grinding pens of us hacks and hackettes. What I had failed to see is the tremendous amount of social work a newspaper does in its daily life. Think for a moment of the Lonely Hearts Column. Now I used to read the Lonely Hearts Column in the *Barnsley Bugle* regularly and it struck me that if Tall Good Looking Prof Solvent Gent Early 40s NS.GSOH.WLTM. Prof Lady Similar. NW., really was as described then surely he wouldn't have to advertise, there would be legions of eligible women camped outside his door every night as though it were the January Sales come early. But Life As We Know It is not like that. I now realise, having perused many and many a Lonely Hearts and Singles Column, that the world is full of ships that are passing in the night and that it is the business of newspapers to make those ships collide so that the bell is ringing at Lloyds faster than Carlo's ice-cream bell and Tiny Tina the Tug meets Larry the Liner of her dreams. It must be difficult, if you're not in some kind of club or organisation or don't have a big circle of friends for you to meet anybody at all, let alone somebody you would like to share your cocoa and duvet with for the rest of your puff.

Hypnotising the Cat

'Samson is looking for his Delilah', one hopeful wrote to the *Llanberis Clarion*, going on to add 'If you too are into wind-surfing, swimming, basketball, rowing, discus, football, rugby, weightlifting, archery and tennis then look no further.' Well Delilah, either you get the scissors out and give him a quick trim or you can look forward to passionless nights spent reading the *Karma Sutra* next to a snoring, throbbing mound that is pumped full of anabolic steroids and smells strongly of Sloan's Liniment.

'When replying to enquiries use your Common Sense', says the advice at the head of the Lonely Hearts Section of the *Guardian* and immediately beneath is the following:

'Vivacious Brunette Aquarian. Of a certain age. NS. GSOH. Own Teeth. WLTM. Solvent older gentleman for country walks and candlelit dinners.' Now that could be a genuinely nice lady wanting happiness and security. Conversely it could be a female Crippen preying on unsuspecting, greying, rich men, luring them to her pied à terre in Royton with mucky talk and promises of bouillabaisse and glasses of chilled Blue Nun. All goes well for a few weeks and the Merry Widow greets them each evening in chiffon and lace, a cloud of perfume around her that would induce asthma in a town. After the will has been signed, leaving everything to her, the poor devils arrive to find that the soup is full of ground glass, and the wine, while still young and fruity, definitely has more than a hint of Paraquat. Still I digress.

I've often wondered what I would put in a Lonely Hearts Column if I were on the loose. 'Scorpio rising, mature, vertically challenged Peter Pan NS. GSOH. WLTM. Wendy with Castle/Brewery/Pub who would like to give a home to his liver.' Well, at least it's honest.

•••••••••••••••••••••••